Scribblings: Diary of a Head Teacher

Tom Panagiotopoulos

PRESS

PRESS

Published by Vulpine Press in the United Kingdom in 2022

ISBN 978-1-83919-172-5

Cover by Claire Wood

www.vulpine-press.com

To the children, of course.

What I really would like said about me is that I dared to love. By love, I mean that condition in the human spirit so profound it encourages us to develop courage and build bridges, and then to trust those bridges and cross the bridges in attempts to reach other human beings.

- Maya Angelou

SCRIBBLINGS
DIARY OF A
HEAD TEACHER

In a time of Covid-19 lockdowns, risk assessments and more information than any head teacher can process, the life of the school goes on. After decades of debate on whether technology will take over teaching, we now have our answer: teachers are irreplaceable. What follows is what a normal school year looks like and will look like again.

Introduction

I was named after my grandfather who wanted to be a teacher. He never finished his studies because the Second World War broke out and he joined the war. The whole family would comment on how much I reminded them of him and since he was the family hero, it seemed like a good fit to follow in his footsteps. I was living up to a myth and I was determined to finish what he had started. I remember lining up my toys and pretending they were my students. I had a little chalkboard where I would write the alphabet and teach my bilingual class for hours on end.

I grew up in the city of Chicago and like so many other immigrants my parents aspired to a better life for their children. They worked hard and expected me and my brother to work even harder to succeed where poverty had stood in the way of their dreams. I was the first in my family to go to university; a huge honour for everyone and a big responsibility for me.

I moved to the UK twenty-five years ago and I immediately began my career in teaching. I spent a few years as a supply teacher moving from school to school to pay the bills and get a feel for what kind of teacher I wanted to be. London was expensive even back then, so I eventually decided I needed to get a permanent position that would give me some job security and pay progression. This is how I came to my school. At first it was to cover a maternity leave, but I was soon offered a permanent position. I have spent twenty years of my life in this school learning about what it really meant to be a teacher. My school is special (but of course all teachers say this about their favourite school).

On my first day I discovered the school was on special measures – a category by Ofsted to describe inadequate schools that are in danger of being shut down. No one had bothered to tell me this at the interview for fear of me running away. I found out after a couple of weeks when a teacher mentioned the upcoming Ofsted inspection in the staffroom. But I was young and enthusiastic and had no fear. This was not going to define me.

The Ofsted category of special measures has broken many people, but the school had a strong leader who was determined to steer it to calmer waters. We hit it off immediately. She was my champion and mentor, and thank God she could see through my rough edges. The years rolled on at warp speed and the longer you stand still in London schools, the more responsibilities you acquire.

It's easy to criticise leaders when you are not the one making the decisions. You can sit back and poke holes without an ounce of accountability. Of course, you would have all the right answers if you were in their shoes, but these answers are more complex when you hold the power and need to find ways to bring people together. I dreaded the day the head teacher would retire because I knew I would either need to make the leap up to the ultimate position or leave the school and start somewhere new. But like I said, my school was special, and I needed to see things through to their natural conclusion. So, I spent ten more years as the head teacher steering the school to those calmer shores, always aware of my destination but enjoying the twists and turns along the way.

My school is in the top 5% of the deprivation index in the UK; this means most of the children are on free school meals and for some of them it is the best and maybe their only meal of the day. I have seen first-hand how poverty can be a defining factor in the life of a child. I have seen first-hand how they struggle to communicate without the words to explain how they feel or what they need. I have seen first-hand how dirty their clothes can be and how neglected their feelings are. I have also seen first-hand how resilient they are despite these obstacles. I have seen their smiles as they come in every morning and show us the day is full of endless possibilities. I have heard their dreams and listened to their pain, and I know this has given my day a purpose. For every teacher that doesn't give up on these children, there are thousands of dreams waiting to be made. We, their teachers, will be their dreamcatchers.

Sharing these stories is like sharing bits of my soul. They might be funny and flippant at times, but it's been a therapy of sorts writing them down over the years and putting them together in this diary of my 'scribblings'. In my first year as a 'civilian' (this is what

I call life post-headship) I anticipated that my daily routine would need to have a structure. Every morning, for the first year after leaving my school, I got up at the same time and spent the first four hours of the day writing my stories down. At the end of every day, C would just check in and say, "Did you do your scribblings today?" That was code for, "I hope you kept busy and didn't get bored." So, day after day I lived through my memories and slowly this book unfolded in front of my eyes. This is a diary of a school year, but full of the experiences of a lifetime. For so many of the children we are their family. Indeed, I always refer to them as 'my children'. I am fiercely protective of them and will cherish their memories as little gems of my existence. I can only thank them for making me a better person.

4 September

First day of term. It's like going back to work after the New Year's celebrations feeling a bit fragile that the holidays are over. No teacher ever sleeps properly the night before being back in school, but now you are the adult, and the Sunday blues are most truly traumatic. I went in super early to get a head start. The school is a one form entry primary school in one of the most deprived postcodes in the country. A one-form entry school consists of one class per year group, and for London standards that is a small school. Visitors always call it an oasis as it is tucked away in between looming council tower blocks. However, over the years with all the gentrification and hipster cafes popping up, if you blink, you might not notice the poverty.

As I approached the gates my body spontaneously took a deep breath; it isn't a conscious one, but my body memory probably kicked in. I had prepared the training day over the summer holidays; it's another round of how to keep children safe in education. Along with this enormous safeguarding responsibility we will need to fill in diaries, agree on marking expectations and set out our behaviour strategies for the year. And all of this in one day. I checked the school answering machine, but there were too many messages to listen to, so I decided to wait for the school secretary to go through those. I made myself a strong cup of coffee and got ready for the onslaught of e-mails.

Here we go…I pressed enter and waited for all the nonsense. I did check them over the summer holidays but stopped two weeks ago to have a proper break. I had 1235 new e-mails. I was tempted to just press the shift key and delete the lot but, unfortunately, I was afraid I might miss something important. I quickly scanned the names and opened only the ones I recognised.

By 9 a.m. I'd heard about fifteen people's accounts of their summer holidays and my response had dwindled to a dry and succinct, "It was great. Thank you for asking," and I walked away just wanting the day to move on to other more interesting conversations than the holiday snaps. By the end of the morning, we had exhausted every possible scenario of child abuse, neglect, and thresholds of making referrals to social services; all very necessary training, but a very depressing backdrop to the start of the school year. We had graphic conversations about what constitutes a serious disclosure and I left the room for a coffee already feeling like the weight of the world was on my shoulders.

The afternoon continued with more exhilarating training on how to provide the most effective feedback to pupils (i.e., how to make our books look good for Ofsted). We colour code our responses, have symbols for different errors and insist that the children edit their work in a different colour. As if asking a child to write another sentence using an 'exciting verb' in green pen will make a damn bit of difference to their progress and knowledge. It's all a very carefully choreographed routine that we must perform when Ofsted and the local authority come in to check. Teachers know that the learning happens verbally at this age, but all the instruments of accountability want to see is written evidence. That's not what the pedagogues say, but this is what we face in a society obsessed with targets and quantifiable written evidence.

The day finished with a review of our behaviour policies. We made the decision to abandon the trust cards we'd previously given children to walk around the school with; this is just a little laminated card with the word "TRUST" written in capital letters and in bold writing. We'd used them to quickly spot which children had permission to walk around the school and which were just doing a runner. This way we knew which ones to question. Staff objected to holding them when children come back from the toilet because they would be dripping wet. We couldn't guarantee it was just water.

Even I had a moment with a 'trust' card. One evening at a bar I dropped one whilst fishing for my wallet to pay for a drink. A young lady tapped me on the shoulder and said, "Excuse me, sir, but you dropped your trust card." I was mortified. I tried to laugh it off and said, "My minders are at the door, don't worry I'm harmless." But she was not amused and just walked away from me with a concerned look on her face.

At 4 p.m. I announced to the teachers that they could have the next day as a planning day and prepare their classrooms. It was the first time they had smiled all afternoon. I think this won me some brownie points.

I went back to my office to continue with the onslaught of e-mails. All the sadistic consultants waited until the first day back to start bombarding us with requests to justify their positions. They start their e-mails with those annoying platitudes of, "Hope you all had a wonderful summer break and have recharged your batteries ready for the new term." Just once I want to respond, "Yes, I enjoyed my holiday and recharged my batteries, so why are you trying to ruin it with your senseless paperwork!" I just ignored them for another day, even though they all 'red flag' them as if the four horsemen of the apocalypse will ride into town if we don't fill in their action plans.

At 6 p.m. I heard a knock on my door and my heart sank. My year 6 teacher wanted to speak to me. I told her to come in and sit down. She told me she has great news and announced very proudly that she's pregnant and will be going on maternity leave in February. These are the moments when head teachers have an immense existential crisis. The human part of me is so thrilled that this young woman will be starting a family but the head teacher part of me tries not to scream, pull his hair out and hurl himself out of the window. So, I smiled and said, "Congratulations, I'm so happy for you!"

What I was actually thinking was: "Where am I going to find a year 6 teacher in February right before the SATs tests? Don't you know that a one form entry school can't afford to lose the only year 6 teacher during SATs? Couldn't you have timed this a bit better and go off in July to have your wonderful bundle of joy? Why don't any of you think of me? Why God? Why am I being punished on the first day of term?"

By 6:30 p.m. I'd had enough and headed home with my batteries not as fully charged as they were that morning.

Happy New Year! Let the games begin.

6 September

The children were back today. It was so wonderful to see their bright and shiny faces in the playground playing with their friends. School is the happiest place in their lives and they had grown over the six-week summer break. I stood next to a boy named Michael in year 6 and he was almost as tall as me. He stood on his toes and we both laughed. He would measure up next to me at least once a week and I couldn't wait for the day he got that sense of achievement that he surpassed his head teacher in some way. He already knew more maths than me, but I hadn't let on that he got the answers faster than I did. I had a reputation to uphold after all.

So far, so good. It's all going smoothly and even the parents were behaving themselves. I could see the sheer joy in their faces as they dropped their children off for the rest of the day, and some until 6 p.m. It's a minefield for those working parents to juggle the responsibilities of work and childcare over the summer break.

The bell rang and the children lined up in the playground. I stood at the stairs saying good morning to each one by name. Parents are always amazed that I can remember all the children's names and even most of their surnames. Welcoming them every morning and making that brief connection is important to me in establishing relationships. Unfortunately, the ones that get most of my attention are the naughty ones, so this is my opportunity to smile and say 'good morning and have a great day' to everyone.

I could see most of them had new hairstyles ready for a new school year. Their uniforms were mostly brand new and neatly pressed, with shiny new shoes that for some were just a bit too big for their feet in the hope that they would last all year. I made a note to some to wipe the crumbs off their faces as they smiled those brilliant smiles and made sure all hats were off before they entered their classrooms. Most of them tried to give me a hug on the stairs, but I told them to keep moving as this would create a monumental jam on the stairwell. It's still the best feeling in the world.

As they all settled in for their first lessons, I went off to check the attendance registers to see which children had not come back. The absentees were still on holiday somewhere in Spain, Turkey, or Nigeria. It's understandable they were absent with the price of airfare; however, they still affect my attendance percentages. Most parents ignored the warnings now and would prefer paying a £50 fine to the local authority than hundreds or even thousands on inflated plane tickets.

At 1 p.m. I got my first fight. Two boys in year four had just had a massive punch up. I gave them both the Darth Vader stare before I went into my office with the teaching assistant to find out what had happened. I came out five minutes later and saw that they were still arguing.

I raised my voice a bit, "I can't believe you have the audacity to continue arguing after what you've just done, and on the first day of school." They looked at me with blank faces. Note to self: don't use the word audacity with a bunch of nine-year-olds.

"This might need to be an exclusion!" I announced emphatically and saw the visible horror on their faces.

Now I had their full attention. They came into my office and told me of the drama of the ball game that went wrong. By this point I could see they had both calmed down and just wanted to get back to class. They were willing to cooperate and take responsibility for their actions. Of course, this didn't warrant an exclusion, but they didn't know that yet. They knew they would need to be punished and so began the negotiations of how severe it would be. They quickly offered to apologise to each other and shake hands completely unprompted. It was going very well.

We decided on no playtime for the rest of the week and I would send a letter home to tell their parents. They didn't like that last bit and I got some tears, but they quickly recovered when I told them I wouldn't be excluding them on this occasion as they had sorted it out and apologised. They seemed happy with this resolution and I sent them back to class. I went to check on them later in the day and they were happily collaborating on an art project and cracking jokes. It always amazes me how boys can have a punch up one minute and be best friends the next.

Now girls are another kettle of fish. They have the emotional intelligence to carry it on for years and years and trying to unravel their conflicts is like holding a summit with well-trained assassins able to knock each other out with just a single flick of an eyelid.

8 September

On my way home I saw an ex-pupil of mine. He was in one the first classes I had ever taught. I recognised him immediately and he was so proud that I could remember his name.

"You haven't changed a bit, Mr P," he said to me.

They all say that, and I hope it's because I'm ageing well and not because in their eyes, we were always old and now they can't believe we are still alive. I was about twenty-eight when I taught him. That was twenty years ago. I calculated that he must be around thirty years old now. He had grown so tall and looked so dapper in his suit and tie.

"What are you up to, Nathaniel?" I asked.

"I'm working in the city," he replied proudly.

"How's the leg?" I asked.

"It's stronger than ever," he said with a cheeky grin on his face.

In my first week at the school, I had the biggest shock of my short career. It was a normal day and my turn for playground duty. It was a lovely crisp spring day, and the children were in a particularly good mood. No fights or accidents to deal with and that was a good thing as I didn't know the school routines very well and the children even less so. It was at this point that Nathaniel kicked the ball and everything went mute and into slow motion. His leg went flying into the air. As I watched his leg turn a few somersaults my mind raced at warp speed.

"What on earth is happening?" was my first thought. Followed immediately by, "What do I do now?"

"What first aid do I administer?"

"How do I reattach his leg?"

"Where's the blood?"

"Call an ambulance now!"

It was the worst horror film I had ever seen, and I was in it! It wasn't until his leg fell to the ground with a resounding thump and bounced for a few feet, did I realise that Nathaniel's leg was a prosthetic. This was way before the days when a very organised Special Needs Coordinator would hand over a massive file for any child with medical needs. It was more like 'learn as you go', and boy was I learning. I ran to Nathaniel. He had already collected his leg and he could see the worry and horror on my face.

"Oh, don't worry Mr P," he said rather nonchalantly, "it happens all the time."

Well not to me, I thought and helped him up to attach his leg.

Once it was attached, he was back in the game. There was no stopping him.

I later learned that it was amputated not long after he was born. He didn't know any different, so he coped well. In class it would itch him, so he needed to take it off. It was at this point the others would hide it and we would have to look for it. To them Nathaniel was just another classmate that just so happened to have a prosthetic leg that they loved to hide. He took it all in his stride and would laugh at me when I would start yelling, "Okay, I'm going to close my eyes and count down from ten and unless the leg turns up, we are not going out to play!" The leg always magically turned up before I would get to zero. Nathaniel never told on them. After a while I started thinking it might have been him doing it, just to wind me up.

He was a remarkable boy, always smiling and it was that smile that made me remember his name twenty years later. He pulled up his trouser leg and showed me his new titanium leg.

He tapped it and said, "Stronger than a jumbo jet."

"I'm sure you could still outrun me!" I added with a smile.

"Do you remember the shock you got when you found out I had a prosthetic leg?" he asked.

"Not only do I remember, but I also retell it at least a dozen times a year. You can't forget something like that," I confessed.

As we said goodbye, he shook my hand, a man now but always the boy in my class.

He said with his brilliant smile, "Thank you, Mr P, for looking out for me."

I immediately welled up and said, "It was my pleasure."

As I walked away, I could feel the tears rolling down my cheek and felt so relieved that I had helped him because I really didn't know what I was doing.

Meeting Nathaniel made me think about what I have learned all these years and in what ways I have changed under the pressures of this continuously shifting educational landscape. Of course, I know more about procedures and policies and how to keep children safe in education. I also think I'm a better communicator and have developed fine diplomacy skills to counteract my natural tendency to just jump in and hope for the best. Even though those times with Nathaniel twenty years ago were possibly chaotic, we all shared a common sense of purpose in teaching for teachings' sake and not for the outcomes expected. Accountability is a great thing until it sucks the life out of the spontaneous and wonderful.

9 September

Fridays are often the days that can be a complete 'shit' show. Last night it rained so heavily I thought the rain was going to come through my windows. I got to school with trepidation as the old Victorian building tends to flood in the basement when it rains heavily.

We are a curious school with four different buildings to manage on a one form entry budget. It's a logistical nightmare. Victorian sewers are not made for global warming.

I opened the doors to the main building and sure enough the whole floor was flooded. As I was walking through the water, I noticed it had a strange brown colour and the smell was pungent. When I spotted a floating turd, I realised this quagmire wasn't rainwater, but raw sewage that had come through the toilets. I promptly turned around and left the building. I took off my shoes and socks and luckily, I had a pair of trainers in my office to wear.

What do I do? I'm just a teacher, I thought for the millionth time in desperation.

I tried not to cry and luckily the caretaker was in, so at least I could talk this through with someone. We called the cleaning company, but they were not allowed to deal with raw sewage. I couldn't blame them. Then I did what any other sane person of the twenty-first century would do. I googled it. There are special companies that deal with this kind of catastrophe and I just called the first one that came up on the search engine. They told me they could come in, but it would cost £5,000 to just walk through the door as everything would need to be ripped out because raw sewage is an environmental health hazard. The man on the phone told me that once they de-contaminated the premises, they would issue me a certificate to present to the council for the school to be used again. It then dawned on me…I would have to close the school down. It was 8 a.m. and some children were already in the playground waiting to go to the breakfast club.

My heart began to race and I could feel the pressure in my head building up as my forehead got hotter and hotter. I ignored the slight tightening of my chest and splashed some cool water on my face. Luckily, the school secretary and one of my older Teaching Assistants are great in a crisis. They immediately started contacting parents to let them know that the school would have to be closed. A million questions raced through my mind.

What about the children who come in by themselves?

The kitchen is in that building and we can't provide lunch. We will need to get sandwiches delivered for those that are here.

How much is this going to cost?

Will our insurance cover it? I have hardly any contingency funds this year. My budget cannot cope.

Is that sharp pain down my right-hand side a stroke?

I'll deal with that later it's not the left-hand side, so I'm not having a heart attack.

I told all the teachers to make their way out to the gates and let the parents know that the school was closed and escort any children lingering on their own to the office. By 9:30 we had about a dozen children happily playing outside. For them it was just a day off school, and they loved it.

The pain down my right-hand side had migrated to my neck and I could feel a new twitch. I took a few deep breaths, just like they had taught us in mindfulness training. I closed my office door, shook all my limbs just to be on the safe side and when I concluded I was just having a panic attack I came back out again.

Luckily, our parents can be very surprising sometimes. They can kick off when their child loses a jumper, but at times like these they are very understanding. Nobody complained and even a few of them asked if we needed any help. This is when you feel like it's really a family. Thank God for small favours.

At 10 a.m. the cavalry arrived. The cleaning crew wore protective suits and masks before they went in to inspect the damage. My thought immediately was, *I can't believe I just walked through all that shit in my shoes.* The man in charge asked if anyone had walked through it and I tell him it was just me and the caretaker, so he took away our shoes and socks for safe disposal. My new Prada loafers in the bin! I was ready to cry. Now this was turning out to be a true catastrophe.

"If I don't have a stroke now, nothing will kill me." My shoe collection is my only luxury in life; now this was becoming personal.

By 4 p.m. they had ripped out everything that had been soiled by the contaminated water, including all the custom-made

19

cupboards which held all our curriculum equipment. Flooring was ripped out and whatever wasn't metal and couldn't be disinfected had to be thrown away. The whole floor was left as a shell. The cupboards alone cost £10,000, so I dreaded to think how much this would cost. Although the true cost was the years shaved off my ever-shortening life.

At 5 p.m. the man in charge of the cleaning brigade issued me with the certificate of cleanliness which meant at least we could open the school on Monday. I thanked him profusely for being so thorough, but I refrained from shaking his hand. I slumped into my chair and realised I hadn't eaten anything since my breakfast at 6 a.m. A few minutes later one of my teachers popped her head through the door and asked me if I wanted to join them in the pub for a 'Friday drink'. All I wanted to do was curl up in a dark corner and rock myself to sleep.

"No thank you," I said.

She cocked her head to one side and asked, "Are you okay?"

What planet do you live on? I thought.

But I guess it was above her pay grade to think about the shit that hit the fan that day. Thank God it was Friday!

12 September

After a relaxing weekend putting all the 'shit' behind me, I came in today feeling more positive. I also had good news that the insurance company would cover the cost of refurbishing the whole basement. It looked like it could cost anywhere between £30,000 and £40,000. The minute you tell a company that you are a school there is an immediate mark up of about 50%. I think there is an unspoken contract of collusion between all these companies to rip off schools. Even though we get three quotes for most work above £5,000, they are all pitching it within the same ballpark figure. It's impossible to get away from this masonic tribe of unscrupulous businesses that think working with schools is a license to print money.

I hate Mondays because they are the most frequent day that staff are off sick. This means ensuring supply staff are called in and briefed so that they have some work to do.

Being a supply teacher in London is a difficult job. You are at the bottom of the food chain; you get abused by children (even the ones that are normally well-behaved), no one talks to you in the staffroom, and you don't know how to get from A to B. By magic you are always the one on the rota for playground duty too. This happened to me as a supply teacher in the early nineties. I remember how exhausting it was feeling totally out of control all day long. I was once asked to teach French to year 10 pupils and all I know in

French is how to order food in a restaurant. There weren't any textbooks, no planning, nothing in the exercise books that would give me an idea of what they were learning, and this was all before the day of the internet and the interactive whiteboards. I thought I would just teach them about life in Paris. I actually stayed there once for a month (it doesn't constitute living there, but it was all I had). They ended up lighting matches and throwing them at me. Unfortunately for them, they lacked understanding that the likelihood of the tiniest flame on a match reaching me across the room was impossible.

My school is completely the opposite. We are so caring and sharing that we bend over backwards to make supply teachers feel welcome, as if we are in some desperate popularity contest to be the homecoming queen. I sometimes worry that it's all my fault and that I've created this insatiable need to be liked. *Oh my god, is it really a reflection on me?* I certainly hope not as I would like to think that I am feared and revered in equal measure.

13 September

A member of staff texted me at 6 a.m. "Sorry but I won't be in again today as H is still feeling unwell and I have to look after him." Great start to the day. When I got in to school, I discovered that the caretaker was running late too.

I went into the hall to prepare for my assembly and a little girl from the breakfast club gave me a lovely flower she had drawn, and it said, "You are the best Head Teacher in the world!" She is only seven years old and has known only one head teacher in her life, but I ran with the feeling of pure adoration from this lovely child as I wanted to stay positive. I thanked her and gave her a head teacher's sticker. She smiled and proudly skipped back to her table to show off her sticker to her friends. I knew what was going to happen next, they would all scramble to get coloured pencils and paper to create their own bouquets to present to me in the quest of that head teacher's sticker.

I pinned her pretty little flower on my display board, and I stepped back and smiled. It was nice to know someone appreciated my work today and they thought I was the best in the world at what I do. This is the beauty of a primary school; from one second to the next the children can lift your spirits.

15 September

It's very unfortunate when communication breaks down between school and family, and then the obvious next step, according to the parent, is for them to move the child to another school. This decision rarely makes any difference. All you are doing is moving the problem from one school to the other and usually at the detriment of the pupil who ends up losing all his/her friends, and the adults that have worked hard to offer support. A fresh start can sometimes do wonders but only if it is planned properly and everyone works towards a common goal.

However, to have a family rock up at the start of the year without being given any information about them is a recipe for disaster, and this is what happened today with a new pupil, David.

I introduced myself to David and extended my hand to him. "I'm the head teacher Mr P, nice to meet you."

He didn't make any eye contact and reluctantly shook my hand and quickly put it away.

I said to him, "I think you're an Arsenal fan."

His face lit up and I could see a brilliant smile. "How do you know that?" Luckily, his Arsenal trainers betrayed him, but I didn't let on.

"I had a call from Arsène Wenger telling me that you are coming to my school today," I replied.

He laughed and I could see that he was missing a tooth. "No, you didn't. I've never met him."

I continued, "He's a bit like Santa, he knows when his fans have been naughty or nice."

David laughed out loud and I could see he was more relaxed now.

"What did he say I am?" he enquired. I'm sure he didn't believe me, but he tested the waters.

"To be honest," I said, "he told me that I should give you a chance to show me your best side and when you do, I will be very impressed."

He nodded in agreement. Maybe he will have a good start after all.

18 September

One would think that the biggest headache in schools are the pupils, especially in urban areas. That couldn't be further from the truth. After all, it is our duty of care to ensure we do our best by the pupils in our charge. However, there are far worse nightmares than a punch-up between twelve-year-olds, and that's a punch-up between their parents. I have had parents scream obscenities at each other, threaten to kill, and even pull each other's hair out in the middle of the playground.

Today, when I came out to the playground at the end of the day, I encountered two mothers who had just finished what I can only assume was an almighty brawl. There was an audience around them watching the whole spectacle and none of them thought to step in and help. They were still screaming and going for each other even though it was obvious that they were exhausted from the altercation, which could have been going on for some time before they even came into the school.

I stepped in between them to signal that this was stopping immediately. I heard one parent in the crowd yell, "Go Mr P." I tried desperately not to raise my voice and give them a piece of my mind, so I just did what most referees do and put both my hands in the air in the hopes that this would get their attention. Luckily, they stopped the screaming and lunging at each other to come up for air.

They looked completely dishevelled. There were even some hair extensions on the ground blowing in the wind; it was carnage. After a few minutes they agreed to come into my office for mediation. I showed them the way and made sure I walked in between them in case they went for each other again.

Mrs Anthony was on my right and she is a formidable figure. She stood at least a foot taller than me and looked straight ahead like a boxer ready to go thirteen rounds. Mrs Brown is the opposite. She is small and fiery and with her tracksuit you could mistake her for one of the pupils. I could see her from the corner of my eye trying to fix her extensions and readjusting her top.

We got to my office without any more arguing and they sat down on either side of the table avoiding any eye contact.

"What's happened, I thought you two were friends?" I asked.

They both started talking at the same time and, worried it would escalate again, I decided to set some ground rules. Just like I would have done with their children.

"This is how it's going to work. You will each get a turn to tell me what's happened without any interruptions. If you cannot have a reasonable discussion with me, then I will have no choice but to ban you both from the premises and report this to the police. Is this clear?"

That seemed to get their attention. They looked like two overgrown teenage girls sulking and Mrs Brown was trying desperately to reattach her extensions. They both nodded in agreement, but I could tell they could blow at any moment. There was a lot of teeth kissing and eye rolling going on.

I asked Mrs Anthony how this started, and she was ready. "Well this 'ho'…"

I stopped her. "Hold on a minute…we will not be using obscenities in my office. If you cannot tell me without swearing, then I will have to ask you to leave."

She readjusted her seat and started over with a relative amount of sarcasm in her voice. "Well this laaaady (the 'a' so long it could have slapped the other one in the face) has been 'sexing' my husband."

I think she thought 'sexing' was more acceptable than bangin', so I let her have that one.

I really didn't know what to say, so I just asked, "Are you sure?"

Big mistake! She whipped out her phone and started reading messages she had copied. *Oh God,* I thought. I didn't really want to hear all the lurid details, but I couldn't stop her. It was like watching a car crash in slow motion. After some graphic accounts of positions, size, screaming and 'hitting the spot' I was lost for words. It was Mrs Brown's turn to tell her side. What happened next shocked me to the core.

"You are jealous of me," she said, flicking what little hair extensions she had left on her head.

This was the extent of her remorse for what seemed clear to me was a betrayal of friendship and trust.

"Is that all you have to say?" She didn't like my questioning and leaned over the table visibly angry. Despite her small frame she is quite fit and muscular, and I thought she was going to punch me.

"Listen Mr P, I don't feel comfortable sitting here talking to you about my private life and I don't need to apologise to her," she said, emphatically pointing in Mrs Anthony's direction.

"I understand completely," I continued, "and under normal circumstances I don't need nor want to know anything about your private lives. Unfortunately, you have brought your private lives into my school and made a spectacle of yourselves in front of all the children and the other parents. Do you understand how embarrassing this is for all of us?"

Since this is way too raw for them to apologise, I suggested what I have suggested thousands of times with the children: that they stay away from each other for the time being and as a matter of priority speak to their children about what they had witnessed today and assure them that it had nothing to do with them.

They both agreed that they didn't want the children to be affected, so at least we found some common ground. I let Mrs Brown leave first as she had the youngest children waiting for her. While I waited with Mrs Anthony, she disclosed to me that this wasn't the first time her husband had done this with someone she knew. She also told me that he had other children with a few women in the area. I could see how utterly devastated she was and looked totally defeated. She now looked smaller than her 6-foot frame. I told her I was so sorry to hear all of this and that she is a nice lady, who didn't deserve this. She apologised to me for the scene she had caused. I knew she was sorry and the look on her face was enough regret for one day. Unfortunately, the true culprit got away scot-free. I wish I could have had him in the room to give him a piece of my mind.

19 September

Another government initiative hit my inbox this morning. This one was about the obesity epidemic. My heart sank at the amount of work this was going to generate and how soul destroying it would be to my staff to tell them they have to do more. So now it's our fault we have obese children in our school. The amount of change we absorb is phenomenal. With every new initiative comes a whole parade of jargon that I can't even keep track of anymore. Once something is announced on the news, it's only a matter of days or even hours that it becomes the schools' responsibility. Half the time I feel like I need a crib sheet just to be able to talk with relative confidence about my own job. If that's not insanity I don't know what is.

A knock on my door snapped me out of my frustration. Luckily, Amy was sent to me with good work. She had written a lovely story about a trip to New York and about all the wonderful experiences she had with her family. I asked her if she visited New York over the summer holidays. She said she had never been there. Initially I felt sad, but I realised that she had tapped into the power of her imagination and somehow managed to go on a 'trip' of sorts. I told Amy how proud I was of her writing and that I particularly liked the way she described the lights at night and used the word 'twinkling' to show that the buildings from afar do look like stars.

I let her choose a prize from my special 'prize box'. Her eyes lit up and when she smiled, I could see she had lost all her top front teeth. She said, "Thank you, Mr P" and I could detect a slight lisp as her tongue popped out in the gap between her teeth. She chose a brilliant pink yo-yo and ran out of my office to show her friends. I could hear her telling an adult outside that she was so happy to have a new yo-yo, and in her excitement, she left her writing book behind.

I turned back to my inbox and promptly closed my e-mails. I decided it's time for my learning walk this week (just a quick walk around the school to check up on the children and see what they are learning). I took her writing book and I walked around the school to see what wonderful work our teachers and children were doing today despite the new initiatives that will never go away.

The PE coaches were teaching archery in the hall, so I went to see how it was progressing. I got to the door and saw a big sign informing me that I can't enter as there is an archery lesson in progress. It's all in red capital letters and I was relieved all the safety protocols were being followed. I waited patiently until one of the coaches let me in and I sat down with the children. Even the timid children were encouraged and supported by their peers to take a shot. One girl was so surprised she hit the target that she punched the air in a sign of victory. I like it when they take risks and succeed.

On my way out one of the coaches asked me if I wanted to have a go. The children loved that idea and started to clap. I didn't tell anyone that I used to belong to an archery club. I pretended to take instructions from the coaches and even asked a few silly questions to make the kids laugh. I took aim, shot and hit the bullseye. The roar from the class was deafening. That was my mike drop moment. I left promptly before they asked me to do it again.

21 September

We had an instrumental assembly today with guitar, piano, and violin. Our uptake is low this year, so the music co-ordinator thought it would be a good idea to get some of the better players to do a mini concert to drum up some interest. The assembly was great with lots of audience participation, especially in the guitar section where they played some classics like, "We Will Rock You" and "Stand by Me". When the violin recitals started, or as I would like to call it 'nails scratching down a chalkboard', I remembered an ill-fated evening about fifteen years before I became a head teacher.

I had friends over for dinner on a school night. By the time I finished tidying up I wasn't sleepy, so I turned on the telly and settled in watching a documentary about the transgender community. The first part was about two women who were in a relationship and had undergone mastectomies and taken testosterone to present themselves as two gay men. Right before the commercial break I caught a glimpse of a naked woman on a sofa with all the characteristics of a man. To my shock I recognised him as our violin teacher at school. He had just started working with us, but I was certain it was him.

I waited in sheer agony for the commercials to finish. Why do they seem so much longer when you are waiting in anticipation? It was him. He'd had similar medical procedures as the previous women and presented himself as a gay man. But what followed was even more shocking. The interviewer was walking with him in Hampstead Heath where he was regularly cruising for anonymous sex at night with gay men.

When the interviewer asked him the obvious question, "What happens if they figure out you're a woman?"

His answer was very simply, "Well let's just say that I've had to blow job my way out of a few sticky situations."

I don't remember the rest of the documentary because by that point I was pouring myself a double gin and tonic trying to erase the image out of my head. What on Earth was he thinking? And then all the existential questions came flooding into my head.

"Do I tell the head teacher?"

"Is it any of my business?"

"Everybody has the right to live their lives without judgement or prejudice as long as he's not harming anyone?"

"What if the parents see this?"

"He works with children, should he be on television naked and talking about blow jobs?"

"Am I being a prude?"

"Will I ever sleep again?"

"How long before the sun comes up?"

"Should I call a friend or a shrink?"

"Maybe I should just ignore it."

This continued until the early hours of the morning and when I gave up on sleep, I just got up and had a double espresso and a shower. I decided I was just going to think about it for the day. He only came in on Tuesdays and it was Thursday, so I had some time to make the right decisions. Later that morning I found myself chatting to the music co-ordinator in the staff room. We were chatting about the upcoming concert when he said to me that I looked tired. I told him I had friends over for dinner and then couldn't sleep, so I ended up watching television.

"Oh yeah," he said, "I was up late too last night with my daughter, she's teething. I was watching telly too. What were you watching?"

"Just a documentary," I replied.

He persisted. "What documentary?"

"Something on Channel Z."

"I was watching channel Z too," he said with curiosity in his voice and then I noticed his eyes widened. It dawned on me that he had seen it too. We stared at each other for a few seconds until the penny dropped completely.

He just blurted out, "Oh my God, you saw it too, didn't you?"

"Yes, and I haven't slept all night," I said, relieved that I could share this with someone, and I flopped down on the seat next to him.

"What are we going to do?" he said.

"I don't know about you," I said, "but I've got thirty children to teach in twenty minutes and need to get them from the playground."

I suggested we discuss it at the end of the day and not do anything rash. He agreed.

By the end of the day, I found him in the staffroom, and he told me that he had just received a message from the violin teacher saying that he would not be back. He apologised and explained that he had filmed that documentary about six years prior and he never expected it to be aired. I suggested that we tell the head teacher, just in case something comes back, and she needs to deal with it. It boils down to the fact that he had presented himself in a state of undress on national television talking about sex in public spaces. I felt sorry for what he had endured, but I think he's probably been brave all his life and will just need to continue.

So here I was fifteen years later, and the children still sound the same when they are learning to play the violin: just bloody awful. We live in hope and I clapped profusely when they finished.

22 September

I had a school council meeting today. There are ten of them (a boy and girl from each class from years two to six). I have a little book for them to ensure that their classmates are writing down suggestions for us to discuss at our fortnightly meetings. It's all very democratic. They were elected by their peers and they sign a contract with me when they join the school council, which outlines their responsibilities and code of conduct. I insist on this as the school councillors can sometimes end up being the naughtiest children in the school. They are always the most popular. They just have the 'x' factor and know how to work a crowd with equal measure of charm and fear.

The representatives from year two went first, and they were nervous. I felt sorry for them, so I offered to read their suggestions and I could see why they were nervous. Most of the suggestions were about longer playtimes, more games in the classroom and a swimming pool. I asked them if they really thought these suggestions were possible and they immediately tried to disavow any knowledge of what their peers had written (although I could recognise the handwriting and the suggestion for the pool came from the school councillor in front of me). He was looking down at the floor by this point trying desperately not to attract any attention to himself.

"Well," I started, "we can't make playtimes longer because we have to teach for a specific amount of time every day. The only place we can fit a pool is in the playground and then where will all the children go to play? As far as the games for the classrooms are concerned, I think it's a great idea to get new board games for when it's raining."

Their faces lit up. I don't think they believed they could get that one through. "Why don't we look online after the meeting and order some games for every class," I suggested. All the councillors were thrilled.

Darren, the year 2 boy said smiling, "That was my idea."

I replied, "Yes I know Darren and the one about the swimming pool was yours too."

He looked surprised. "How did you know?"

I looked at Darren mysteriously, went close to his face and replied in an ominous voice, "I can read minds." He quickly put his hands on his ears as if that would stop me entering his mind.

I could see I won this one. They truly felt like they had made a difference, they would return triumphant to their electorate. I was going to ask the teachers to order some games anyway, so we were all winners. Now let's see what they have to say about their learning at the next meeting.

I got home at 4:30 today and C thought something was wrong.

"Why are you home so early? No disasters, no child protection issues, no staff meltdowns, no building problems, no police; just a normal day of ABCs and 123s? So, you did your proper job for once," was the reply with a wry smile.

"Yes, that's right," I said, laughing.

I shook my head in utter disbelief that it could be that easy sometimes, but utterly complicated at the same time. As I took a shower I wondered if tomorrow I would pay for this relatively 'normal' day.

23 September

I came out of the school hall today and saw two police officers questioning an ex-pupil in front of the gates. He comes every day to collect his younger sister. A crowd of parents had gathered around the police and were asking questions. I could see that the officers were getting irate at the public's questioning and were asking them to leave. When I reached the gates, I could see the boy was visibly anxious at this 'cornering' and I addressed him first.

"Are you ok T.J.?" I asked him but he didn't respond. He just kept his head down and didn't make any eye contact.

One of the police officers said to me, "Go away, mate. We are questioning this young man." And he put his arm out to stop me from approaching the boy.

Mate? Did he just call me mate? I thought in utter indignation. My blood started boiling quickly.

Well, that was enough for me to step on my angry citizen soap box and launch at him.

I ignored his outstretched arm and headed straight for T.J.

"For your information *mate* (and I emphasised the mate rather menacingly) I am the head teacher of this school and this is one of my ex-pupils who comes every day to collect his sister. He is only thirteen years old, even though he might look older, and unless he has done something illegal, I suggest you leave him alone and stop

41

creating a scene in front of my school gates. This is embarrassing for all of us."

The beefier one stepped in and came closer to me thinking that this would do the trick and he said, "The family are known to the police and we just have some questions for him."

What on Earth does his family have to do with him? I thought.

I immediately responded, not backing up an inch.

"I don't care what his family are known for, he is only thirteen years old and doesn't deserve to be intimidated in this way, so I suggest unless you have probable cause to detain him further (I got that one from watching Law and Order) you let me escort him to his sister's classroom. I will also be contacting his parents to tell them that this has happened. So, unless you want this to escalate, I think you should let us all go on our merry way because I am certain you aren't allowed to question him without his parents present."

By this point I was certain I would be arrested and escorted off my own school premises in handcuffs, but miraculously they got on their bikes and left us alone. There was a huge crowd gathering around us making sure they got the best seat in the house. A few parents clapped when the police got on their bikes and congratulated me for helping the young boy. They started patting me on the back and all I wanted to do was get the T.J. away from everyone. I could tell my street cred had gone up with the local community.

I quickly took him to the office to get him away from the crowds. While we waited for his parents, I asked why they stopped him, and he said they probably thought he was one of his older brothers who has got into some trouble recently. I told him not to worry and that he did all the right things. His response was so nonchalant that it shocked me to the core.

He said, "It's not the first time, Mr P, I'm not worried and I know what to do when it happens."

24 September

After yesterday's incident with the police, I wondered if any of my current pupils have faced similar stops. I asked the boys in year six who are between eleven and twelve years old if any of them have been stopped by the police and most of them put their hands up. They told me stories of how the police make them take their shoes and socks off and check them for drugs. They thought this was normal. Some even laughed and thought it was a badge of honour to have been stopped and searched in this way. I was horrified.

After work that day I made my way to the local police department. I was determined to speak to a senior officer and share my findings and concerns. I waited patiently for about twenty minutes and to their credit I was given my time to share the children's experiences. The officer was not very forthcoming when I asked him why he thought this was happening and I was not going to get him to discuss with me my opinions on racial profiling. However, I did discover that anyone who is stopped and searched should be given a form by the police. He gave me a bunch of these forms to show the children back at school, so they know what to expect if they are ever stopped again. I felt uncomfortable with this. I wasn't sure I should be preparing them for this kind of life. It's telling them that this is inevitable. On the other hand, it's being pragmatic and equipping them with knowledge and power to defend themselves.

When I look at my nursery children, I can see early on how their socio-economic background is already carving a path for them. Our job is to try and divert them from this path. It all starts with their limited communication skills. Poor language means poor relationships and poor relationships means even poorer emotional intelligence leading to a lack of empathy and understanding of the world, making them more vulnerable to stereotyping and bad choices. What are the solutions? It requires our leaders to have more hope that society and people can change. However, belligerently questioning a thirteen-year-old black boy, not because he has done anything wrong, but because he is part of a certain family or fits a certain profile, is certainly contributing to the problem and perpetuating the stereotype of the poor black child having a higher propensity to illegal activity.

These are not messages of hope and love, but fear and loathing. I decided to share the forms with them in the hope that their knowledge will give them power and be a force for change in the future.

26 September

My alarm didn't go off this morning! I didn't have time for coffee or breakfast and just ran out of the house. I hate being late. I made it in at the same time, but at the expense of my morning rituals. I usually get up at 6:00 to start my day without getting my pulse racing. It is the only time of the day where nothing can bother me. I wash my face, brush my teeth, and then sit on the edge of my bed to breathe for ten minutes. It's not so much meditation as much as an opportunity to check in with myself and my body. Over the years I have had to learn how to stop and allow myself to just relax and breathe.

In the middle of my tenure as a head teacher I had a huge wake-up call one day, which shocked me to the core. At the time I was doing three jobs: I was a head teacher, an Ofsted Inspector, and a local authority School Improvement Partner. On top of it all, someone had just tried to burn my school down.

It was a Friday afternoon at a big event with hundreds of people in the hall and a pupil reported to me that his classroom was on fire. I ran upstairs and discovered a fire raging in a bin dangerously close to a display board. I kicked it over and tried to smother it with a jumper, but as I lifted the jumper, the plastic from the bin along with the flames stuck to the jumper and fell on my head and burnt my scalp and neck. I stomped on the remaining flames (there goes another pair of shoes) and finally put it out. Thank God it was only just some cosmetic damage to the floor. The funniest moment came when, in the wake of the smoke and the burnt plastic, I looked over and spotted the fire extinguisher just two feet away from me. What an idiot!

I spent the whole weekend worrying about who had done it and whether they would try again. By the Sunday morning I woke up and the right side of my face was paralysed and lopsided. I went to the hospital and even though I could move my arms and legs I was convinced I was having a stroke.

Once I told the receptionist my symptoms, I was rushed through A&E and within fifteen minutes was hooked up to an ECG and had two consultants examining me. Thank God for the NHS. It really works. It turns out I had Bell's palsy. The doctors asked me if I have a high stress job or if I have gone through any trauma recently.

"Well, where do I begin?" I told them. They stopped me before I wound myself up again and really had a stroke.

I was signed off from work for two weeks so that the steroids they were pumping into my body could reduce the deterioration of the nerves and I could regain movement.

So, what did I do?

Two days later I went into school to chair a meeting about a building project and I announced at the start of the meeting that I might be drooling as I could not feel the right side of my face. I spent the rest of the meeting cleaning up spittle from my mouth and pretending I knew what they were talking about. Again, what an idiot!

Having a health scare is a good message from the universe to take stock in what is essential to having a balanced life. I had tipped those scales so far to the side of work, that I rarely noticed the exponential rises in my stress levels until the damage was done. At least it wasn't permanent.

28 September

We had a School Council meeting today and the children were on top form. To be honest, I also use them as my little spies. I surreptitiously ask about behaviour just in case something has evaded my learning walks. You would be surprised the nuggets of gold I get out of them. We have a code of conduct and we don't name and shame, but I know immediately who they are referring to when they complain about someone's behaviour. However, sometimes you take their complaints with a pinch of salt because children can be extremely punitive when given a little bit of power.

Today I asked the million-dollar question: What do you think about your learning? I never ask them what they think about their teachers, because that's not what I want them to focus on. We all have different teaching styles and sometimes the most popular teachers are not the most effective.

I told them that I had put £1,000 into a school council budget and they are responsible to spend it on behalf of the children of the school. They were apoplectic with joy. They thought it was a fortune. Wait until they figure out how little that can buy them. I turned it into a project for them to research and cost up. I asked them what they thought we can do with this money. Darren put his hand up and blurted out, "Build the swimming pool!" He finally thought this was enough money. Here was his chance for his dreams to come true. The older ones laughed, and I told them off. He looked sad, but I patted him on the back, and he brightened up. I admired his tenacity.

Another one said, "Take all the children to Disneyland."

"Okay," I said, "how would you work that out as a maths problem?"

Malik, who is a bit of a mathematical genius, said, "Well you need to decide how long you are going to stay and then work out how much it will cost for one person and then multiply that by the number of people going."

"Absolutely right," I said to him and he beamed.

There's nothing more satisfying than that smile they have when they know they are right.

"So, Malik you are in charge of costing this up and reporting back to the school council," I announced.

They were all so thrilled, but I could tell that Malik already knew that it was impossible, but he relished the authority of reporting back to me. He was already taking notes and making plans. He came to me almost daily to discuss his ideas. And I know that by next week I will have a power-point presentation and handouts.

I also tasked the others to prepare a presentation and have it ready for the next meeting. Hopefully, there will be some realistic options from the older ones to choose from.

29 September

Today, Sandra in year 3 made a disclosure that her father beat her with a belt and a wooden spoon last night. At these moments, the school goes on high alert. It's like pulling down the shutters and waiting for the hurricane to hit. I immediately referred it to social services.

By midday I had written twelve pages of notes and I was waiting for the police to arrive to interview the child. The police usually request for a member of staff to be present during the interviews and that inevitably is me. Over the years I have heard some harrowing accounts of physical violence and emotional abuse. She had a series of bruises and visible lashes from the belt on her arms, legs, and back. The police took photos and copious amounts of notes. They were exceptional; very well-trained and professional.

When the father arrived, he was immediately brought into my office by the class teacher. You see on these occasions we remove the child from the classroom and make sure she/he is safe in another part of the school. The police officers explained the situation to him. They were two young female officers, and he was getting very agitated. He also wouldn't put his phone away even though they asked him a few times to put it on the table. He was known to the school for being a hot head and now my worry was that he would start kicking off and it would not be easy to restrain him.

He repeatedly refused to put his phone away and was constantly checking it. As he was not cooperating, he was told that he was being arrested and that he would have to hand over his phone and be handcuffed immediately.

Great! I thought and all in my office within spitting distance of children and parents.

He leaned over and said to me, "Are you happy now, Mr Head Teacher, you got me arrested." He was sitting next to me and there was no way I was going to get away from him.

You must be joking! I thought.

I lost my temper and I stood up to confront him. When I got up, I realised he was still taller than me even though he was sitting down. I had not thought this one through, but now I was committed to my moment.

I launched into him pointing in his face and in my strictest head teacher's voice said, "I wasn't the one that put the belt in your hands, mate, and repeatedly hit your child and threatened her if she told anyone. How dare you blame me for being arrested! I suggest you cooperate with these officers and begin by apologising for your despicable behaviour. Now hand over your phone and stop acting like a child."

The officers had called for back-up, but he surprised everyone and gave the phone up. He also began to cry. They put the handcuffs on him, and I asked them if they could refrain from doing that as he would be seen by other children and parents on the way out. They couldn't, so I took my jacket and put it over his hands so that the handcuffs were not visible. I went outside to check how many people were around and got one of the teachers to move some families on to the back of the school so that they wouldn't see him.

I went out with him to ensure he was okay and before he got into the police car, I took my jacket off his hands. He looked defeated at this point and rightly so. We didn't speak and they closed the door.

The police officers thanked me for my support and one of them said, "You should come work for us, you were great at diffusing that situation."

"I'll keep it mind," I said and wished them luck.

I guess breaking up a fight between angry children in the playground isn't much different from dealing with immature adults. However, the children have rarely hit back and that's one thing I don't think I can risk. Sandra went home with her mother and at least for tonight she will be safe. That's all that mattered.

I went back to my office and one of my teaching assistants had kindly made me a fresh cup of coffee. "I'll need something stronger than that," I said to her and couldn't wait to open that bottle of wine waiting for me at home. After spending another hour writing it all up and filing it away, I went home and cracked open that bottle immediately.

"How was your day?" C asked.

Do I describe blow by blow what happened and spend the next hour reliving the drama or do I just say, "Same old drama," and let the glass of wine wash away the horror? I did neither. I just let the tears run down my face. C immediately knew it was a bad one and just enveloped me in a hug. There was no need to say anything.

3 October

In autumn, the whole school mobilises itself for the annual harvest festival. As a church school it is particularly important for us to celebrate these festivals as a community and pass on important messages to the children. By the end of the month, we try to get all the pupils to donate some dried goods to present at the church service and we donate them to a local food bank. It is exhausting, but well worth the lesson taught to children that no matter how little we might think we have, there are always others that have even less. Is there a better way to ensure our children are becoming responsible citizens than teaching them that they should love one another above everything else? I fear that a lot of those messages are lost when they leave the school gates and are bombarded with images on social media.

However, when I see my pupils, years after they have left us, I think they have kept that beautiful sense of humanity we instilled in them. I can see their love for our school, and it makes me joyful to know we have left a positive mark on their hearts. So, I continue to collect the harvest goods year on year and break my back to display the thousands of contributions the poorest children in the country have donated to those that might need them more than them, knowing this is where I have made a difference.

This year I decided to get a group of children to help me collect all the food and load the car. After some time, I noticed that one group was not as quick as the others. I asked one of the other children where that group was and I found out that they were taking a detour with some of the bags into the playground and eating the biscuits. I told the others to go back to their classes and quickly headed to the playground. I found them hiding behind the huge oak tree fighting over a pack of chocolate digestives.

I raised my voice: "I can't believe what I'm seeing!"

All the bags and biscuits went flying in the air and they quickly pointed fingers at each other. There was no getting out of this one. The crumbs were on all their faces. I marched them into my office, and I could see they were shaken up. But I wasn't sure if it was because they were worried about the consequences, or they were embarrassed by what they'd done. I quickly realised it was the former. I had a long chat about the consequences and told them they would have to donate any treats they got at home to make up for what they had eaten.

One pupil asked, "Can I just buy some more with my pocket money?"

"That's a really good suggestion," I said. I gave it a few seconds to let them think they got away with it and then informed them, "I'll suggest that to your parents when I call them."

The penny dropped. This is where Mum and Dad will let them know the value of sharing with those less fortunate.

4 October

One of my teachers was in a panic that her class hasn't donated enough for the Harvest Festival.

Oh my God! Is this what we have been reduced to? I thought.

"Will you come in and speak to them today and remind them to bring in donations?" she asked with all seriousness.

"Of course, I will," I said enthusiastically, not wanting to disaffect a good teacher.

I put it on my 'To Do list' and did it in the afternoon when they were all rehearsing their play for the Harvest Festival. I don't know how many more times I can stomach hearing the story of 'The Giant Turnip' or 'The Little Red Hen'.

We are having lesson observations this week and all the teachers are on edge. I keep on telling them that it's not about their performance, but what progress I can see in the children's books. However, it doesn't change the fact that you are being observed doing your job and that is personal. I worry more about the ones who aren't nervous at all and downright cocky. They usually are the worst teachers because they have an inflated ego. I took my observation pro forma and headed off to my first lesson. It's a science focus this week and I was incredibly nervous.

Science was never my strong subject even as a student. I remember once teaching a year 6 science lesson about materials that conduct electricity and I had cobbled together some items from the kitchen to show the children. I asked them if the objects were good conductors and how we could test that. There is always a clever child in the class that inevitably knows more than you and likes nothing more than to prove that you are a fraud. I had one such boy named James, who was the naughtiest child in my class, but also a scientific genius. I always imagined that one day he would either discover the cure for the common cold or threaten to unleash chemical warfare on London if he wasn't given a billion pounds. I have yet to hear from him.

At this point I picked up a steak knife with a wooden handle and asked the children if this knife would conduct electricity. Some said yes because they immediately saw the shiny metal and assumed it would let the electricity pass, but I then drew their attention to the wooden handle and asked them how that would affect the current of electricity. Of course, James already knew the answer, so he didn't bother to listen to me until I said the magic words:

"Yes, the wood does not conduct electricity so even if I were to stick this knife into the electrical socket nothing would happen to me."

I regretted it the moment the words came out of my mouth. I wasn't sure this was true and being the assassin that he was, James knew this too. Suddenly, his interest was piqued, and he raised his hand to ask a question. I desperately pretended not to see him, and I tried to move on and distract him, but he was persistent because he wanted to see me fry.

When he could take it no longer her blurted out, "Go on then!"

"Go on what, James?" I said innocently, hoping this would go away.

"Go on, stick the knife in the socket. You have to prove your hypothesis," he said, triumphantly throwing my own teaching back in my face.

"I will James once I have finished showing you all the materials I have collected, and we have discussed their properties," I said feeling more and more unsure of my own knowledge.

"No do it now!" he said looking around the room for supporters in his quest to turn me into fried bacon.

By this point I had some droplets of sweat collecting at the edge of my nose and my ears were getting hotter and hotter.

"Please Mr P, let's see the knife in the socket," piped up a few others.

It was too late now, and my reputation was on the line, so I had to follow through with my stupid hypothesis, but now nervous of the outcome. Why didn't I plan this lesson better? I always want to give them a 'hands on' experience. Next time we are watching a video. No one will die that way.

I took the knife and headed for the socket hoping for the best. I made a full disclosure before I stuck the knife in: "Do not try this at home children." At the last minute I noticed one of the sockets had been switched off and went straight for it obscuring the switch with my free hand. Victory! I did it and James was none the wiser. Coming back to my desk with a round of applause, I could see that James was baffled at my success and his face was full of disappointment that I was still standing.

A week later I retaught the lesson, this time having prepared my materials and I set them straight: "I made a mistake, children. You never stick a knife in the socket."

5 October

David has had a bad start. He is an incredibly angry young boy and I worry about his mental health. We have not received a diagnosis yet and that's because the process has been halted as he has moved schools so many times.

At the end of the day, I could hear loud yelling outside my office. I popped my head out and saw that David had been sent to me. I asked his 1:1 teaching assistant, Frank, what happened, and he couldn't explain to me because David kept on disagreeing with him and interrupting rather loudly. We employed Frank a year ago to work with small groups of children in year 6, but now he's attached to David almost all day. Frank is so patient and caring with the children, I wish I could train him as a teacher and keep him, but his heart is in acting and he dreams of a life on the stage and screen. There were parents and children going in and out of the main office and I needed to get David away from the audience. I asked him to come into my office to discuss what happened, but he refused and started yelling at me. He did this on purpose just to get a rise out of me, so that he could justify escalating his responses. But he always finds a way to wind himself up even if you shut up and say nothing.

I turned away from him hoping to diffuse the situation, but he used this as an opportunity to throw a massive pre-emptive strike.

I'm not even sure if he knew what he was doing, but it was highly effective.

He began screaming at me, "Look at you, you don't even care what happened. You are just believing the adults and walking away from me. That's not fair. You people are all the same."

I gave him the benefit of the doubt and came back to speak to him. I kept my voice calm, but I could feel my own temper rising as he continued to yell at me. I tried to keep my cool as I had a lot of little children waiting to be collected and they were on the table outside my office playing with the Lego.

I reminded him to keep his voice down and stop yelling at me. This made him even angrier.

"Why do you people always tell me to stop yelling? This is how I talk. What's your problem? I hate this fucking school."

At this point I did raise my voice and told him to stop swearing. I also informed him that his mother had been called and he needed to wait here for her to collect him so we can discuss what happened.

He lost it. He picked up the table and tossed it across the hallway and started kicking all the chairs. The two children waiting to be collected started crying and luckily, they didn't get hurt by the table or the chairs. I got them into the secretary's office while Frank and I tried to calm David down. Frank put his hand on his back to slow him down but David swatted it away and just went and sat in a corner. At least he'd stopped kicking the furniture.

At this point his mother had just come in and saw him visibly upset. We all finally went into my office to discuss what had happened. I explained to his mother what had just happened. She asked him if this was true (as if I have nothing else better to do than make stories up and cause myself all this grief). He accepted his behaviour but tried to excuse it by saying that we always blame him for everything. This is where his mother showed him that he doesn't have to accept responsibility for his actions and said to us, "You people keep telling me he's difficult, but you're not getting him help. It was the same in all the other schools. I keep hearing that he's got special needs, but I can't help him."

There was some truth in what she was saying, and I know how difficult it is for parents to cope with children that have extreme behavioural problems. However, in this instance I had diverted so much money from other projects and other children to give David a 1:1 teaching assistant to keep him safe and engaged. I put him at the top of the list to be observed by the Educational Psychologist as a matter of priority. He's only been with us for a few weeks and we have no extra funding for him.

I told her all of this, but she couldn't listen to me because in her head the system is all the same and we are a continuation of the previous school. Unfortunately, there is a fundamental lack of trust on her part that anything can change because she is expecting others to change it for her. She does not understand that it is only in partnership that we can help him and calling us 'you people' immediately sets the tone of us against them.

I refrained once again from excluding David because this was not the answer. When he had calmed down, he accepted that he was out of control and apologised for his behaviour. This was enough for now. I told him tomorrow is another day and he will have a fresh start. He smiled at this and maybe he was more hopeful for the next day. This has not been a good one.

After they left, I went out to check up on the little ones that witnessed his aggression and found a very irate parent waiting to complain about what her son had witnessed. I asked her to come into my office and off she went. I think she yelled at me for about ten minutes and I let her do it hoping that would suffice. Thankfully, it did.

I didn't come out of my office until it was dark and I was sure no one else was in the building to bother me. I noticed there was a full moon.

6 October

We recently acquired a very neurotic couple who took their son out of a neighbouring school because, and I quote, "We didn't want him to sound like the other children."

What the hell does that mean and what did they expect they were going to find here? I told them that the schools are almost identical, but the mother insisted that the children at the other school were swearing too much and she didn't want her son to be exposed to that vulgarity.

Wait till she hears my lot swearing like lorry drivers, what will she do then? I thought.

It didn't take too long for the e-mails to start arriving with complaints. Initially it was why her son couldn't get a place on an after-school club even though she knew there was a waiting list. I responded to her diplomatically and respectfully, but last week she started complaining about the staff.

She has complained about a teaching assistant, the learning mentor and two class teachers. Today she came to see me to complain about homework and brought her husband with her. She has refused to bring her son into school until we promise not to give him any 'time out' if he doesn't do his homework. This was the third time she had withdrawn her child from school over something she disagreed with. She was rude and condescending spewing out her 'philosophies' of education and child rearing and pretended to know more about education than I did. Maybe she should re-evaluate those philosophies the next time her son throws a tantrum at home and she calls me to speak to him on the phone to get him to calm down. She informed me that they don't believe in punishing their children if they did something wrong and we needed to respect their wishes.

I can't wait until those children become teenagers!

I took a deep breath and decided to push back today. Enough is enough and she was just being a bully. I told her politely and respectfully that schools have rules to run smoothly and that she needed to respect and trust our judgements, otherwise our relationship would fail. Furthermore, her behaviour towards my staff had been belligerent and just because someone says no to her doesn't mean that they were being rude or aggressive.

"Sometimes you just need to accept no for an answer and I'm sorry to say in this instance we are the educators. We will just have to agree to disagree and carry on," I finally declared to her and waited for the bomb to drop.

Her husband had not said a word this whole time and at this point his head whipped around in her direction waiting to see how she would react. I think he was pleased someone had politely and respectfully stood up to her.

To my surprise she acquiesced, though she stated, "I will be monitoring this."

"You do that, now, just get out of my office and let me get on with my job." I didn't say as much, but I was profusely sweet and just tilted my head in show of sympathy and said, "I understand that raising children is a profoundly complex experience and I'm sorry you have felt this high level of anxiety. I'm here for any clarifications you may need in the future and hope we can continue to work together for Michael's sake."

She really didn't know where to go with this and by this point, I was standing signalling that this meeting and all her nonsense was over. I shook the father's hand and wanted to wish him luck. She was too busy looking at the messages on her phone to shake my hand. No doubt she was waiting for a response to another complaint.

At the last minute I reminded her that Michael needed to be in school the next day, otherwise I would be referring them to the Education Welfare Service, and they could be issued with a fine. I could tell she didn't like this ultimatum, but we were dealing with a woman who had never heard the word 'no' before. I closed the door and uttered a sigh of relief.

I could hear her outside having a go at her husband for not saying anything during the meeting and I felt relieved that she had moved on to someone else.

10 October

I went out with some friends last night and had a bit more to drink than usual. I try not to go out on a Sunday night, but it was the only time we were all free. My morning rituals were slow today and I thoroughly regret that last round of cocktails. This was so much easier twenty years ago.

In my morning haze I recalled a comment one of my friends made, which really struck a nerve with me. She said I point my finger too much when I'm talking, like I'm scolding everyone or trying to make a point. I am very self-conscious of this now.

"Do I really point my finger a lot?" I need to remember to ask C tonight if I really do this.

"Or maybe I should call now and ask?" I was obsessing again. I'll just try and observe it during the day. I would hate to think that I have turned into one of those caricatures of a head teacher that pedantically points at everyone.

It was a beautiful sunny morning; one of those crisp days where the trees are wearing their autumnal hues. I walked through the park and purposely stepped on the piles of dried leaves to hear that crackle under my feet. It brightened me up and I could feel the coffee kicking in and the hangover dissipating in the fresh air. When I was a child, I used to love jumping into piles of leaves with my brother. It is one of the fondest memories I have of my childhood.

I stopped short of skipping but couldn't help but feel some euphoria today. I stopped off at my coffee house where everybody knows my order and my name. It's a bit like *Cheers*, only without the alcohol. The lovely barista told me I looked smart today and I could tell she was flirting with me. It's nice to feel desired. Or maybe she was just being nice? "No, no she's definitely flirting," I convinced myself of this as I took my cappuccino and headed for school.

There were two massive foxes on the roof of the nursery building and as I walked through the gates they stopped and looked at me. I worry one day that upon arrival they will have taken control of the premises, take my keys and shake me down for my money. I kept walking, trying to make as much noise with my keys as I could, but nothing seemed to deter them. *They are getting way too comfortable and too expensive to get rid of.* Our exterminator said that men's pee makes them go away. I think my job description stops short of urinating around the premises. Maybe I'll just point at them.

12 October

Luckily, today nothing major happened until lunchtime. Maybe the gods have taken their mercy upon me. But that thought quickly dissipated when one of my teachers came in to say the magic words, "Just to let you know…" This was where my day changed its course completely. Julien had disclosed that his mother hit him on the arm. I spent the next few hours on the phone to social services and the parents. Mum admitted to hitting his arm, but that's because he was in the middle of pulling a pot of boiling water off the hob. I finished all the investigations by the end of the school day. The cut-off point is the end of the day because I never want to send a child home with any doubts about their safety. In this instance we all agreed that the mum was under a lot of stress and we would be offering support and just monitoring the situation.

Early on in my career I realised how skilful people were at passing the proverbial 'buck' on to me and the phrase 'just to let you know' was the easiest way to get rid of that hot potato.

For those of you that are not in leadership roles, this is code for: I have told you and this is your problem now and I will disavow any knowledge or responsibility for the issue, so do your job and deal with it because I will not bother.

Once at a staff briefing, I asked with irritation in my voice, "Why wasn't this problem followed up with the parents?" The staff member involved quickly retorted, "I did let you know last week when we spoke on the stairs." So that quick, 'Just to let you know' on the stairs at 1 p.m., was the point in time when I became responsible for dealing with an issue involving a parent and a member of staff. That was the exact point in time when as far as she was concerned, I was fully briefed on the issue and had all the relevant information and would magically solve it as the omnipotent and omniscient being that I am. Are you kidding me?

The following week I officially banned the phrase and told staff that under no circumstances do I want them to pass on information to me using the phrase 'Just to let you know'. However, people very creatively found replacement phrases to get what they want. So very quickly, 'Just to let you know' became 'You might be interested in…' Help me.

Currently we have two strands of tummy bugs – one produces violent vomiting and the other explosive diarrhoea. Schools can be laboratories of germ warfare. Children seem to just incubate all the viruses and then come into school with a vengeance to unleash mayhem.

Most staff have been ill this week. I had three supply teachers in today and for a small primary school that's a quarter of my staff. Children have been projectile vomiting left and right and we have changed numerous soiled uniforms of those who didn't make it to the toilet in time.

After I sent home Julien with his mother and put away all his safeguarding notes, I was left with a child who felt ill and was waiting for her mother to collect her. Suddenly, I could see that she was turning a dangerous shade of green.

She is going to hurl, I thought, and I needed to stop her before she did it on my new carpet. I grabbed the bin and sprinted towards her. I made it just in time to stop the vomit from hitting my carpet. Unfortunately, it was my face that stopped it from hitting the carpet. By the time I ran to the toilet to stick my face under the tap I was vomiting too. I don't think I will ever wash that memory from my mind.

13 October

Today we had the School Council presentations for the £1,000 budget. As predicted, Malik had prepared a PowerPoint presentation and a handout with all the costings. He was wearing a jacket and finely pressed cotton chinos with his church shoes on. He stopped short of wearing a tie today. He started very formally:

"Good afternoon fellow councillors. I am here today to present the budget for the proposal of the whole school going to Disneyland for three days."

The first slide was a picture of Mickey and Goofy with the £1,000 at the top. Mickey and Goofy were smiling. The second slide had a picture of the Eurostar and the French flag. I'm so pleased to see that they have learnt how to do a PowerPoint presentation.

"As you can see from my slide, I have chosen Euro Disney.

"I spent some time costing this up for you and looked at various travel websites to compare prices," he continued with an air of authority in his voice and quickly readjusted his jacket collar.

Malik was being very thorough. He'd even using cross-curricular skills with the costings and the data handling.

"The full cost for one person is £450. For three hundred people at £450 each… (he was presenting this very well and even had the figures transitioning into the slide one by one until his final reveal) the total cost would be £135,000."

At this stage there was an audible gasp in the room. It even shocked me how much it would cost.

Malik continued, "This doesn't even include travel insurance, which I'm sure Mr P would want with so many children travelling?" He immediately looked at my direction for validation.

I nodded looking impressed and he smiled. He had thought of everything. I couldn't have been prouder. The last slide had a photo of Mickey and goofy with sad faces. There was a collective "Ah" in the room.

14 October

Jacob, a boy from year 6, was sent to me because he punched someone during a football match. A few years ago, we began a programme of study on mindfulness for children, so we are all about using calming down strategies to avoid conflict. From their very first lessons the children learn about the main parts of the brain and how they are affected by emotions flooding their brain. They learn about the 'amygdala' (the oldest part of the brain that reacts when we are in danger).

I asked Jacob why he hit the other boy and he said, "Well, he tackled me on purpose and my pre-frontal cortex didn't have time to calm me down, so my amygdala punched him."

He had a triumphant look on his face, which signalled, "I have given you a scientific explanation as to why I can't control myself and you taught me this, so I can't be punished."

It took everything I had not to laugh and lose all my credibility. To top it off I could tell that Jacob was enjoying this immensely as he had the most sardonic smirk on his face.

I asked him in all seriousness, "Who needs to be punished? You or your amygdala?"

He looked at me perplexed, not knowing how to answer the question. The smirk quickly vanished, and he wrinkled his brow.

I got you now, I thought.

But Jacob is very clever and without hesitation he said, "I think I have learned my lesson, but my amygdala needs a time out." He ended this sentence sounding like a question. He was pushing his luck and he knew it.

So now I was going to be punishing a part of his brain he didn't think was his problem.

I was determined to teach him a lesson. "How do you think your amygdala is going to have this time out?"

He looked at me and I could tell he had nowhere to go with this one.

He said with annoyance, "I will have to come with my amygdala to the time out."

"Good idea, Jacob, and maybe you can invite your pre-frontal cortex along and get to know him a bit better than your amygdala. Or better yet, maybe you should introduce them to each other, so they can work together in the future, so you don't find yourself in this position again. And by the way, I will be calling your amygdala's parents to let them know this happened. Maybe they can help him calm down." I smiled at him.

His face was like thunder now at the thought of his parents being contacted so he said, "What if my amygdala has a whole week's time out and I join him, can you then not call his parents."

I considered his offer, but then remembered we did the same song and dance routine a few weeks ago.

"I'm sorry, Jacob, but I don't negotiate with amygdalas, only pre-frontal cortexes," I declared.

I think he got the message.

On his way out he said in one last ploy to reprieve himself, "What if my amygdala apologises?"

"Well then," I said, "that's a whole different story."

His face changed and I could detect a smile of hope.

I continued, "Then this will be a good start for your amygdala to be forgiven."

He nodded in agreement knowing that it could have been worse. He left with his head down and his smart-ass revolution squashed.

17 October

It was time for my regular walkabout. I do it to see what experiences we are giving the children and to check their books to see the progress they are making. Some teachers are never concerned when they see me in their classrooms, but others are terrified.

The children love seeing me and they are always keen to show me their work. They know they will get a sticker or a special prize if the work is outstanding, so they fight for my attention. Today I told them I was invisible, but I could still see them. I would appear when I was ready to talk to someone. They seemed to accept this and stopped trying to get my attention, but I could tell their eyes were on me and they were desperate to get me to sit with them.

After about twenty minutes I made my way to a table that was working very diligently on their story writing. I made myself 'appear' to them and started asking about their writing. At this point I noticed the little boy sitting next to me had wet himself. I made a big deal about his writing and told him quite loudly to come with me to my office for a prize. This way I could get him out without anyone noticing. When we came out of the classroom, I told him I knew he had wet himself and not to worry. We went and got some spare tracksuit bottoms from the lost and found box and I gave him a plastic bag to put his wet clothes in. When he came out of the toilet, he looked visibly brighter. I asked him why he hadn't gone to the toilet. He said that he was waiting for me to 'appear' at his table.

"I was desperate and couldn't wait any longer," he continued.

I felt horrible.

"I'm sorry, Ben," I said to him.

"It's not your fault, Mr P. I should have gone to the toilet, but I was excited to show you my writing," he said.

I pulled out a fantastic performance and made him feel special.

With huge gusto and bravado, I said, "I liked your story so much, you can have one of my super-duper special prizes under my desk."

We went to my office where I always have a stash of special prizes and I pulled out a remote-controlled car. He started screaming and jumping up and down. The tracksuit bottoms I gave him were so big he had hold onto them with one hand.

I said, "Thank you for waiting for me to see your writing, but next time it's more important for you to go to the toilet and then ask your teacher to show me your work. You don't need to wait for me to come to your class."

"Okay," he said, but I doubt he heard me as his eyes were glued to the car.

"Come back at the end of the day and I will give it to you," I said.

I couldn't run the risk of him going into class with the car in his hands. If the others thought he got this because he wet himself, it would be nappies all around.

We forget how little our children are and sometimes in the whirlwind of pushing them to succeed we forget that they need nurture and care beyond the classroom. Moments like the one Ben just had can be very traumatic, but we always make sure we counteract them with immediate moments of kindness.

Hopefully, Ben will remember feeling special on the day he wet himself.

19 October

I love assemblies. You might say I'm a masochist because most head teachers dread them, and most adults have endless memories of the tediousness of the head teacher incessantly preaching to them. However, I think of it more as an opportunity to perform to my audience.

Today's assembly worked a treat. There is nothing that annoys me more than litter. I see it everywhere: on the streets, in the parks, on the buses and trains and even in my own school. We are living in a disposable culture and this is reflected in our streets and public spaces. Children see people eating on public transport and discarding the waste on the floor or on the seat next to them. They grow up with the idea that public spaces are huge waste bins.

So today I went for the shock factor. I prepared my assembly before school and filled a bin with paper and containers. I washed and dried everything in preparation for my performance. I also collected some wrappers, paper and fruit and put them on a table next to me. As the children were coming into the hall, I was peeling a satsuma. They were all looking at me curiously as to what would be coming next.

Once they were all seated and ready to listen, I said, "Excuse me children, but I just need to clear my table."

I proceeded to throw all the rubbish on the floor in a very deliberate and dramatic fashion. It was flying everywhere and there were gasps in the room. Shock, horror and awe. They couldn't believe I was throwing all this rubbish on the floor.

I just looked at them in surprise and said calmly, "Why is this so shocking to you?"

They gave all the right answers. But theory and practice can sometimes be worlds apart. I continued to litter as I talked to them and I could tell that this horrified them. I then told them the story of my bus journey the other day and how I had to sit amongst discarded chicken bones and takeaway containers and sweetie wrappers.

"It was a little bit like this," I said, picking up the bin that I had stuffed to the brim with 'clean' rubbish and emptied it into the crowd.

What followed can only be described as pure chaos. It was carnage. The teachers were desperately trying to calm them all down. I let them scream and wriggle and feel the sheer horror of all this rubbish around them. Once they calmed down and we picked up all the 'rubbish' I told them it was all clean and handpicked by me for the assembly. Otherwise, I would have parents lining up after school to crucify me.

I showed them pictures of my journey into work today. I took close ups of all the rubbish I had to navigate to get into school. It ranged from paper to bottles to quite messy dog poo, which got the loudest response. In our discussion they admitted having thrown rubbish. Some said there aren't enough bins on the street.

81

"That's not true!" I said emphatically. "And even if it were true then put it in your pocket and throw it away at home."

Then one child piped up, "But there are rubbish collectors paid to pick it all up!" He got a few pats on the back from his mates for his answer.

Now we are getting somewhere! I thought.

"Okay," I began, so I gave him an analogy. "So what you are saying is that it's okay to litter on the streets because there are people paid to collect it. Is it okay to start fires because there are people paid to put them out?"

The children were horrified at this thought. "No," they all say, "because it's illegal and someone can get hurt."

"Well, I'm sorry to inform you," I continued, "but littering is illegal too and you can be fined and go to jail." (A bit of an over-exaggeration as law enforcement has bigger fish to fry, but I needed to get my point across.)

I finished triumphantly by telling them that I needed their help in this fight to stop people from littering and I would make them all superheroes in this quest. "Your mission," I said, mimicking the mission impossible theme, "if you choose to accept it...is to stop any family member or friends from littering. If you see them, remind them to throw it in a bin. Come and report it to me and I will speak to them personally."

I realised at the end of the day that this was a big mistake when one little boy came up to me at the gate with his mum and announced that she had just thrown her can of coke on the street. She could have killed him. I was trying desperately not to laugh and explained to her that we had an assembly today about stopping people from littering.

I tried to make light of the situation and said to him, "Well maybe mummy dropped it by mistake, she has so many things to carry."

He immediately responded, "No she didn't because when I told her she said the street cleaners will pick it up."

There was no saving face, so I quickly told him how pleased I was that he had learnt the importance of keeping our public spaces free of litter and I walked back to the office quickly before he could humiliate his mother any further. I could hear her yelling at him. I chuckled to myself thinking she bloody well deserved that dressing down.

TGIF – and it's half-term too. Every so often I put a pearl of wisdom on the board in the staffroom. It's just a way to communicate something deeper to the people that work so ridiculously hard every day to improve the life chances of our children. Every day I tell them all to have a good day. I thank them for special events. So today I gave them a poem by one of my favourite poets Derek Walcott as a reminder to them to look after themselves over the half-term break:

Love After Love

The time will come
when, with elation
you will greet yourself arriving
at your own door, in your own mirror
and each will smile at the other's welcome,
and say, sit here. Eat.

You will love again the stranger who was yourself.
Give wine. Give bread. Give back your heart
to itself, to the stranger who has loved you
all your life, whom you ignored
for another, who knows you by heart.

Take down the love letters from the bookshelf,
the photographs, the desperate notes,

peel your own image from the mirror.

Sit. Feast on your life.

It's easy to forget oneself in this job, especially as vocations like these can be thankless ones. We are expected to achieve more with less at our disposal. We are constantly asking our teachers to move those goalposts even further. We don't pay them more money and we don't give them more time to complete these seemingly impossible targets. Yet they somehow manage the impossible. They are true heroes that have been forgotten by this rotten system of targets and initiatives. They have had their status ripped out from under them and I worry they will be viewed as being glorified babysitters. Yet they still reinvent the wheel daily and continue to offer love and care even to those that turn around and criticise them because they didn't do it to their satisfaction. They continue to bear the brunt of annual targets, performance management, observations, scrutiny by Ofsted and the local authorities.

As I reflect on the end of this half-term, I hope one day, as Derek Walcott says, we will be able to sit and feast on ourselves and if we do, I hope we can recognise the people we have become.

24 October

Half-term this week. Woo-hoo! I spent the morning in school catching up on all that paperwork that's been piling up. I don't think people realise how much paperwork is involved in education. The e-mails alone are enough to drive you potty.

Whilst leaving the building, I realised that schools are strange places without the children in them. Whenever I go in during the holidays it seems like I can always hear the echo of their voices, a bit like an abandoned amusement park. These places are meant to be filled with people, sounds and movement. When they lie empty, they are sad, so I went for a long walk in the park. The air was crisp, and the sun was shining brightly. I love autumn. The colours are dramatic. I remembered that the clocks go back this week and it filled me with dread that the darkness will settle in for the winter; go to work in the dark and come home in the dark. I wish I could just hibernate and pop up like the blossoms in March.

31 October

Happy Halloween! I don't dare say that in a church school as it offends some parents to even mention goblins, demons, and witches; as if they're not all in the bible in the first place. Wasn't Lucifer a fallen angel turned demon? What better Halloween gore than the passages from the Old Testament. Now I don't have a problem with either of these two ideals. They are both acceptable as cultural phenomena that exist through the ages. What I do take great umbrage at is this e-mail from a parent that just hit my inbox:

Dear Mr P,

I am writing to complain about the homework that Ms Lyons sent home with the children. On the top right-hand corner, you can see a witch flying on a broomstick with a black cat against a full moon. I can only assume you are promoting Halloween at the school, which is an abomination in the eyes of the Lord. This is a church school, and you should only be preaching the Lord's words and celebrating in images pure and divine. I cannot send my daughter to a school that promotes witchcraft and satanic practices. As the bible says in Leviticus 20:27 that anyone who practiced witchcraft, soothsaying, sorcery should be killed.

I sincerely hope you act immediately and stop these unchristian practices, or I will be reporting you to the governors, the church and the Diocese and your job will be in jeopardy.

Sincerely yours,

Mrs Williams

I read it a couple of times to make sure it wasn't a hoax or early April Fool's joke. I showed it to the vicar of the school, who said to me I was free to respond in any way I saw fit, just as long as I didn't swear. He knew me well. So, I sat down and drafted what I thought was one of the best letters I had ever written to a parent:

Dear Mrs Williams,

Thank you for your letter and bringing to my attention the homework that was sent home the other day. I assure you as a church school we do not celebrate nor promote Halloween, although we must all accept that most families do choose to take part in this cultural event as it is fun for the children to dress up and meet their friends for 'trick or treating'. However, I agree with you and have spoken to Ms Lyons, who as a new teacher in a church school, was unaware that this could offend some families and I'm confident it will not happen again.

More importantly, I would like to take this opportunity to address the tone and content of your letter, which I can only assume was written in haste. You have made a sweeping generalisation about our 'practices' from one such insignificant oversight from a newly qualified teacher. I can categorically assure you that we do not 'promote witchcraft and satanic practices' and if you are not convinced, I invite you to come in and spend some time learning exactly how our Christian values underpin all that we do.

Secondly, I do not appreciate the quote from the Old Testament that you used in your letter, which clearly states that we should be killed. This is not only unchristian of you, but also illegal to threaten someone's life and professional integrity just because you are upset. Thirdly, I would like you to know that I have shared your letter with my governors and the diocese. They were all in agreement with me that your tone was unacceptable.

In future I suggest you just approach the teacher in the first instance, who could have cleared this up in a matter of minutes for you and saved you unnecessary anxiety and time in writing to me.

I hope this clears everything up for you, but if you do not feel satisfied with my response, then I suggest you write to the chair of governors and explain yourself further. As a Christian myself and a head teacher in a church school, I find that forgiveness is the best way forward.

I look forward to your apology.

Kind Regards,

Mr P

I took a risk at writing this letter, but she needed to be pushed back. You can't go around threatening people.

1 November

'Rabbits'. When I was in secondary school a very beloved English teacher of mine, Ms Davis, would always write the word 'rabbits' on the board on the first day of every month. She told us that our month would be full of luck if we said this as our first word. To this day I remember to say or write rabbits as the first word of every month. But more importantly I remember Ms Davis. She was one of my favourite teachers. She was a tough cookie and when she got angry at anyone messing about, she would throw the chalk straight at them. A few times she even threw it at me for talking. It never really hit anyone. I think she would just aim at the wall above our heads for maximum shock factor. It would smash against the wall and shatter into tiny pieces. The most that would happen is that we would get covered in white chalk dust. She would probably have lost her job if she did that today, but this was the eighties. Nobody really cared as long as you didn't kill anyone.

So, the adage is true. "Nobody forgets a good teacher", but nobody forgets a bad one either. Let's call her Mrs Beaver. She was the nastiest, most miserable, and smelliest teacher I ever had in primary school. And I mean smelly! Worst thing was that I had her for two years in a row. She was one of those old schoolteachers that never got up from her desk and ruled the class with an iron fist from the front. We never had fun. She never got up from that massive derriere of hers and whenever she wanted to see our work, she would call us up one by one. It was horrendous. We had to hold our breath for the duration of the visit to 'the DESK'. I'm sure we could all have had a career as deep-sea divers after those two years. I think I could hold my breath for about five minutes by the end of her tenure as my teacher. It was just a miracle that I never had to sit near the front. Thank God for my 20/20 vision.

As a head teacher, I always judge the teachers I recruit on whether any of the children could ever turn around and say that they had a bad teacher like Mrs Beaver. Now there are some teachers that are born to teach, others that learn how to do it in varying degrees of success, some that have the best intentions in the world but just lack the 'x' factor and can't control a class, some that think they are marvellous but are dull and ineffective and then there are those that just don't like children and think they should bend to their will. Those teachers are the worst ones and thankfully I only ever had one of those in my school. They can get far because they are very clever, but the children never have a good word to say about them. You can tell how insincere they are when they put on that fake smile when they talk about children and proceed to put their hand to their heart as if this proves they have one.

All I could do is wait for this particular teacher to leave and thankfully that day arrived. A few years later at our summer fair, a lovely grandmother of an ex-pupil came to say hello. She was reminiscing about her grandson's time at our school and sure enough she asked after this teacher. After hearing the teacher moved on to another school, she said, "Teachers should at least like children, shouldn't they?"

I didn't respond. She said it all.

3 November

First thing this morning a child in year 3 threw up on the stairs going to her classroom. Why do some parents insist on sending their kids to school when they are so unwell? All I need is for this patient zero to create a superspreader event. My attendance will plummet. I didn't ask Karen, one of our teaching assistants, to clean up the mess (she's done enough for me). I got the mop and bucket and luckily one of the dinner ladies saw me and offered to clean it up. I just tried to direct the children away from the mess and hoped nobody would tread on it. It was hope in vain. When I turned my back to speak to another member of staff, about ten children had trodden all the way up three flights of stairs and into their class-rooms. I got another bucket and mop.

7 November

Children love collecting little bits of junk in their pockets on the way to school. They are like magpies; straight in for anything shiny or strange. Today Charlie brought in a hubcap from an old car and asked me to keep it safe for him until the end of the day. He loves anything having to do with cars. Last week I made sure I ordered some books on the history of the motor car industry. I was hoping I could use his fascination with cars to get him interested in history.

When I asked him what he was going to do with it he said, "Dunno, it might come in handy one day." I suggested he could use it when he does his science topic on the solar system and it could possibly form part of an installation. He looked at me with a blank stare and then in all seriousness said, "You're funny, Mr P," and he walked away laughing and shaking his head at my suggestion. I'm glad I was able to amuse him, but I was dead serious.

The most extraordinary find came by a girl in year 5 one morning. I was the deputy head of the school and I was having one of those 'Jack of all trades' days covering for absent staff. It was during playtime when a group of girls came up to me in floods of tears to report to me that Mary was going around the playground stabbing people with a syringe.

The questions came flooding in.

"Did I hear right?"

"A syringe? Oh my God!"

"Where is she?"

"What has she done?"

"Where did she find it?"

"How many children has she stabbed?"

"Why didn't I spot her doing it?"

"How can I spot her when I'm on my own with a hundred children all running around?"

"Find her…find her…find her…"

I told the girls to go inside and get another teacher to come out immediately. Then, I spotted Mary trying to hide in a corner of the playground. When she saw me coming towards her, she ran into the toilets and locked herself in a cubicle. That was the best thing she could have done. I had to wait for back up anyway. At least now I knew she was contained and couldn't hurt anyone else. I think the group of girls were quite vocal about what had happened to them, so within a few minutes all the teachers from the staff room came rushing out into the playground. The cavalry had arrived.

A few minutes later the head teacher arrived too, and I was so pleased to see her. She was a very calm and patient woman and great in a crisis. She always had your back. She went into the toilets and retrieved Mary quickly and we took her and all the girls that were stabbed into the head teacher's office.

She tried to prick several children but only succeeded in catching her number one nemesis and she broke the skin. The others were wearing thick jumpers and the syringe didn't go through. *What the hell do we do now?* I suggested we call the NHS helpline to get advice as the needle was probably used. As I suspected the NHS said we had to immediately contact the parents and have the child taken to A&E and be given anti-HIV medication as a precautionary measure.

This was massive and it so happened that the child that was stabbed was the daughter of one of our most difficult parents. Beverley's mother was a formidable character who resembled the cast of *Prisoner: Cell Block H*. When I taught Beverley, the mother got so angry with me once that she announced that Beverley's father was due out of prison in a week's time and he would sort me out. I just responded rather sweetly, "I look forward to meeting him." Mary and Beverley have hated each other since Reception class and so did the parents. The fallout could have been epic. I drew the short straw of having to make the phone calls to both parties. The head teacher was dealing with the children and talking it through with them; she was good at that.

How do you start this conversation on the phone? The phone call to Mary's mother was straightforward.

"Hello Mrs Samuels, I'm sorry to inform you that Mary has picked up a syringe on the way to school today and stabbed seven children with it. This is serious, and you need to come to school now."

She was shocked. "A what!" she said.

"Yes, you heard right a syringe and the head teacher is with her now. You need to come and meet with her," I finished.

The other phone call was trickier. What do you say to a parent who has dropped off their child to school, expecting she will be safe, to hear that she has been stabbed with a syringe? My heart started racing immediately as you cannot help but feel somehow responsible for everything that happens to them in your care. Short of frisking them at the gates I don't know how we could have avoided this one.

As the phone was ringing, I was willing it to go to voicemail, but after the fifth ring I heard her raspy voice on the other end in the middle of a coughing fit. I could tell she had a fag in her mouth too.

"Hello, Mrs Collins, I'm sorry to bother you during the day, but Beverly was stabbed with a syringe today and you need to come in to school and take her to A&E."

What came next shocked me to the core.

"What's going to happen to the other girl? Is she going to be excluded?" she immediately enquired.

It's amazing how most parents are mainly concerned about the punishments that the other child will get. How could you at that point think of the other child's sanctions? Surprisingly, she isn't the only one. Most parents ask this almost immediately. If the other child gets excluded, then they seem to be okay with whatever happened to their own child. It's bizarre psychology to be interested more in some warped sense of justice, than the well-being of your own child. Well at least she was calm about it.

After the phone calls I joined the head teacher in the meeting with all the girls. It was mostly self-explanatory; she picked up the needle on the way to school, put it in her pocket and when the opportunity arose, she went trigger happy. This animosity had been brewing outside of school for ages as Mary and Beverley live on the

97

same estate and have seen their mothers argue constantly. It seems like they are playing out a version of their mothers' feud. The head teacher tried to resolve the issue with some restorative conversations about showing empathy and remorse for what had happened.

The bottom line was that Mary got a week's exclusion, she had to write an apology letter to Beverley, and she missed all her privileges in class for a month. Some people might say that she should have been permanently excluded and I'm sure some staff members would have been saying that behind our backs. However, she wasn't such a bad girl and didn't deserve to be sent to a pupil referral unit where she could have ended up in worse circumstances.

It's easy to make judgement calls when you're not the one holding the ultimate responsibility. Luckily, the parents came at different times and they were relatively calm about the incident. Mary's mum didn't say much, but I could tell by the look on her face that she was going to let it rip when she got home. I was starting to feel sorry for Mary as I know her mum is not easy to handle.

Beverley's mum on the other hand seemed very put out that we had to bring her into school in the middle of the day. She even debated on whether she should bother taking her to A&E and I said immediately that if she didn't, I would. We had a moment of staring each other down and I could hear the theme tune of many good western showdowns in my head, but I won this one.

It turned out that I had to go with them anyway, as I had to hand over the syringe to the hospital. It was an uncomfortable ride in the taxi, but luckily, I passed the syringe on to a nurse relatively quickly and made sure I reported what had happened. They were seen to immediately and I made a quick escape. I looked at my watch, it was 3 p.m. I'd had no lunch, no coffee, no toilet break, and I had to go back to school and deliver a training session on reading. Wonderful. I couldn't even read my own name by this point. I made sure I picked up loads of biscuits and chocolates to bribe the staff and get them on a sugar rush. That distracted them.

"Mr P, Mr P." Charlie must have been standing there for ages calling me, but I was deep in thought by this point. He came back to get his hubcap.

"Have you had any more thoughts about what you are going to do with it?" I asked.

He shrugged his shoulders and looked impatient to get on with his afternoon.

"Maybe you could use it to make a shield for your history topic on the Romans?" I continued not really knowing when to give up.

He shrugged his shoulders again and this time with more energy to signal how unimpressed he was with my suggestions. I handed him the hubcap and he quickly left my office, but before he got to the door he turned back as if he'd had an epiphany and declared, "Maybe I'll just leave it as a hubcap and decorate my room. It's a classic."

"That's brilliant," I said to him and refrained from referring to Marcel Duchamp and the *objet trouvé*.

8 November

At lunchtime I sat with the children to eat and chat about the food and how their day was going. It just gives me an opportunity to see how they socialise and for them to see me in a more informal way. Suddenly, there was a tap on my shoulder, and I turned to see one of the girls in year 3.

She whispered in my ear, "Tony is selling drugs in the playground."

"He's what?" I replied.

"He's selling drugs in the playground," she repeated just a little bit louder. Luckily, nobody on the table heard her.

"Thank you for telling me," I said simply and got up to investigate.

When I started working as a teacher a more experienced colleague once told me to stop dealing with every petty little problem the children have as they have to learn to sort out some problems on their own. I wasn't sure how to do this, so I asked her to explain. She told me all I need to do is quickly assess in my head how serious it is from 1-10 and if it's not over 5, I simply say to them: Thank you for telling me. In this way they feel heard, and you can see if they can be independent and sort it out themselves. Sometimes children just need a nudge to take risks and assert themselves because always trying to solve every petty squabble takes away some of their independence.

On this occasion, however, the seriousness was at 10 and 'Thank you for telling me' was just so I could distract her and get out to the playground.

I tried not to panic as this could be a misunderstanding. I quickly spotted Tony with his friends on the far end of the playground. I walked slowly so that I didn't alert him to anything. Once he spotted me, he quickly stuffed something into his pocket and walked away. I called him over and asked how his day had been. This was not unusual as he had a support plan for his behaviour, which all staff were aware of and followed up. He told me everything was fine and even said he got a certificate for good behaviour. I sounded excited and asked him to come to my office for a head teacher's badge.

On our way to my office, he seemed jovial and relaxed. I even began to wonder whether what the little girl had reported was true. I had already briefed one the teachers in the playground to chat to the other boys in the group, so I could speak to Tony on his own and see what he had to say. If he didn't tell me the truth, then the others would sing like canaries.

I took out the head teacher's badge, but I didn't give it to him immediately. I just put it on the table.

"Tell me how you earned your certificate," I said.

"I followed my targets this week and didn't get angry when I was out in a game," he said.

That's a good result, I said to myself and hoped what was going to happen next wouldn't spoil all the hard work. I took a deep breath.

"I noticed you stuffed something quickly into your pocket when you saw me, I hope you didn't bring your phone into the playground again." I thought this was a good way to focus on whatever he was concealing.

He was adamant. "No, I promise."

"That's good, but was it something like sweets or anything else you shouldn't have in school?"

At this point he put his head down and I could tell he was going to shut down. This is what he does when he knows he's done something wrong and if not handled properly he would have a meltdown. This is the point where I have so many choices at my disposal which will determine how this is solved.

Before I could proceed there was a knock on the door. It was the teacher that had spoken to the other children. She quickly told me (out of earshot from Tony) that he had flour in his pocket and was telling the others that it was cocaine.

"Thank you for telling me," I said to her, now judging the scenario at 10+.

I thought at this point Tony knew that his time was up. I sat back down and said nothing. I took a deep breath. Tony was still looking down at his feet. I chose to tell him I knew everything and see how he responded. His response would determine the consequences, he knew that. It was actually part of his support plan and I reminded him that. To my pleasant surprise, he took out the bag of flour and put it on the table. He admitted to everything apart from the part of trying to sell it. He said that it was just a joke. I asked him how he knew about this drug, and he told me that his older brothers were watching a film and he saw it too and thought it would be funny to pretend.

I didn't ask him what film he saw, and I hoped it wasn't *Scarface*. It's so hard sometimes to decide how to proceed. He had been so good recently and this one thing could send him backwards. At the same time, I have a duty to him and the others to keep them safe and teach them valuable life lessons. I knew he wasn't trying to sell them anything as the others confirmed his story.

I told him this was serious. He nodded and started to cry. I could sense this response was genuine and not just an act to get out of trouble. I was more confident of my decision now. I told him I was going to call his parents and inform them. He agreed this needed to happen and didn't react badly. I also told him that I had to call the other children's parents because they might report the incident at home, and I had to alert them and tell them the truth. I explained that I wouldn't identify him, but I couldn't guarantee that the other children would do the same. He needed to understand that there are consequences to his actions.

Once the phone calls were made, we had a long chat about drugs and safety. I just wanted to make sure he had seen it in a film and not in the home. I logged everything for safeguarding purposes and called children's services later in the day to just check that I followed all the correct protocols. I asked him what he thought his punishment should be. He said he should be excluded for a week. That was not a solution in my book. I told him I think a better way of correcting his mistake was to do a project at home about drugs safety and show it to me in a week. He would also miss some of his 'choosing' time on the computer. He seemed happy with that.

On his way out, I gave him the head teacher's badge and asked him not to wear it right away but wait for another moment when I caught him being good.

"But I've been bad," he said.

"You earned this for good behaviour. That hasn't been erased just because you made a mistake. You took responsibility and helped me solve it. Keep it in your pocket to remind you to make the right choices."

He smiled and I sighed, feeling that I might have made a difference to his life today.

9 November

There is usually a lull in the day around 11:30. At this point I slip out of my office with my lunch and sit in a corner of the school garden where I can see everything, but no one can spot me. It's the only sanctuary I have in the school, apart from the toilet. However, I did have a member of staff follow me once into the toilet wanting to continue his conversation with me. It wasn't until I told him I needed to use the loo, and would he please leave that he even realised we were in the toilet.

Being a head teacher is like being a parent. For the children I find that perfectly natural, but there are adults who need just as much support and guidance as children. It wasn't until I started this job that I realised most people are vulnerable and seek security from their leaders.

Some people just like being told what to do and feel safe with a confident and decisive leader. Others want to suck up endless amounts of your time by passively aggressively seeking validation for every little thing that they do. Those are the most exhausting ones to manage as their need for constant attention is a bottomless pit. They can also get sulky and despondent if you're not feeding their insecurities. I just love the ones who get on with the job, show initiative, come to you with solutions to problems and are emotionally intelligent human beings.

That's the perfect job description for any employee. However, these people are few and far between, so that's why I need to sit in my sanctuary for fifteen minutes every day, to just breathe. I mean deep breathing to the pit of my stomach, where I can get all those muscles relaxed and lower my blood pressure. It doesn't matter how long the sensation lasts, because I can usually guarantee that when I come back something will have happened.

Sure enough on my way to a lesson observation the school secretary informed me that Laurel had been bringing in some of her mother's jewellery and giving them out as gifts to staff. Turns out this had been happening for quite some time. I knew that the school secretary had a good relationship with the mum, so I asked her if she could call her to investigate. Sometimes the head teacher is not the best person to sort out the problem as parents can get defensive with authority figures.

I saw an outstanding lesson in year 6 and came back refreshed to hear the news about Laurel's crime spree. For the last year she had been bringing in gifts at Christmas and the end of year to teachers and teaching assistants. We always assumed that most gifts were cosmetic jewellery, but on this occasion some of the items were real. Her mother reported that Laurel had some problems with stealing and that she was seeing a psychologist about it. It seemed to be linked with some other problems at home. I'm glad I asked the school secretary to speak to her as I don't think I would have got much out of her. The class teacher offered to speak to Laurel at the end of the day and we would collect all the jewellery from the staff for Mum to pick up. I couldn't help but wonder if any of them were diamonds.

11 November

My assembly today focused on peace as part of the Armistice Day celebrations. However, I could not focus on peace without referencing its antithesis. I had prompted a member of staff to interrupt me during the assembly and disagree with me. I gave that job to one of my scarier teachers.

She got up halfway through my presentation and called out, "This is rubbish Mr P. I think sometimes war can be a good thing. It can solve problems that go on for years."

You could hear a collective intake of breath from the crowd as the children's heads went back and forth to see how this was going to pan out. I calmly got up and asked Ms Jones to come to the front and join me.

I said to her, "Thank you for your opinion, Ms Jones, however I don't think you needed to use the word rubbish. There are better ways to disagree with someone without insulting their ideas."

The children were making noises to indicate that I was giving her a dressing down. I could see them flicking their hands and smacking their legs in glee that they were witnessing this.

Ms Jones then continued in the same way, "But it's my opinion that your ideas are rubbish and I have the right to use whatever word I want."

Now the children were in shock that she continued in this belligerent way. They were squealing in delight to see this conflict between a teacher and the head teacher. Some of them were jumping up and down in anticipation for what would come next.

I stood my ground and continued, "Of course you do, but I think an educated person like yourself could use a better word to get your point across. Why don't we agree that you think my ideas are wrong and then try to prove to me that they are wrong by giving me good examples."

I could hear a collective "wooo!"

The conversation continued and we involved the children in the debate over *War and Peace*. In our modern Tolstoy drama, we managed to find some common ground. Ms Jones apologised for calling my ideas rubbish and she agreed that peace is what she wanted, but understood why people have gone to war, especially when they were oppressed and trying to survive.

But that is a revolution I tell her, and war is something totally different. The children were brilliant at spotting the strategies I used to resolve my conflict with Ms Jones and not escalate it. One of them even spotted that I had immediately taken control by asking her to come up and stand next to me, rather than yelling across the hall.

"Why was that important?" I asked him.

His answer floored me. "That's the point you stopped her from antagonising you."

"Great word, Benjamin!" I added.

"It was in my spelling list last week," he said with such pride.

I looked over at his teacher and she was beaming. We can be satisfied with the simplest things in this job.

14 November

I went on a trip today with one of my classes. It's a rare occasion I can go out for the whole day, but some parents let us down and I couldn't spare any staff, so I had to go with them. The children were thrilled that I was coming with them. We were going to Kew Gardens and it was a beautiful sunny day, so I was looking forward to it. On the train one of the girls asked me if I had ever been to Kew Gardens. I told her I had gone there once with my year 6 class when I was a teacher.

Unfortunately, I have not been able to show my face there ever since, I thought, and I was immediately transported to that ill-fated day about twenty years earlier.

I had the most difficult class in the school, and they had gone through two teachers by the time I arrived. The school was on special measures and no one had taken them out on a trip all year. The staff were demoralised, and the children were out of control. They were branded the juvenile delinquents. But I was ambitious and idealistic and ready to take on any challenge thrown at me. I was going to make a difference and do what others had failed to achieve. I was going to be their "Oh captain my captain".

I had planned the trip with military precision and visited the previous week, so that I knew exactly what we were going to do. The purpose of the trip was an extension of our science topic on plants. We were going to learn about tropical plants and do some sketching. I told them if they behaved, we could have a picnic near a beautiful pond and feed the ducks. They could bring some money because there was a gift shop if they wanted to buy a souvenir. It was all going well.

That all changed when Hannah came up to me in one of the greenhouses and presented me with an orchid she had picked. "This is for you, Mr P, thank you for bringing us here." She was so happy and proud to have picked the most beautiful and rarest orchid she could find to show her gratitude. I didn't know where to hide and I looked even sillier holding this orchid in my hand.

What the hell do I say to her? I thought.

Her face was the epitome of joyous splendour.

How can I crush her sentiment by telling her that she cannot and should not pick the flowers? I quickly ushered them out fearing this trend would spread and I surreptitiously threw the orchid into a bush.

The day just went from bad to worse. We were asked to leave the pond area as they were throwing rubbish in the water (they hadn't had my assembly on litter) and some of the boys thought it was funny to try and feed the ducks chewing gum. I was mortified. I was trying desperately to keep my cool, but the rage was building up in every trickle of sweat on my brow. Finally, we got to an open area and I thought I would just let them run off all the energy they had.

As I flopped down exhausted on the grass another school came to join us. This was a 'blazer' school with insignia and all. The children even wore those silly caps on their head.

The teacher sat down and announced in her very clipped and posh queen's English, "Children, I'm going to sketch the pagoda if anyone would like to join me?"

They all beautifully assembled around her with their sketchbooks and began to sketch in earnest. I looked over and saw my lot chasing each other with sticks around the same pagoda. I wondered if they were going to include them in their sketch and describe the wild and crazy things they saw on their trip today. But as I looked longer, I noticed a stark difference between the two groups. Mine were laughing and shouting and screaming their heads off as children should be doing in an open space, while the others were pretending to be adults before their time. I much preferred my children.

At the end of the day, we went to the gift shop as promised and they went mad. Some had quite a bit of money to spend and were intent on spending it all. It was so nice to see that they wanted to buy gifts for their family and friends.

On the train journey back one of my naughtiest boys came to give me a gift. "I saw you looking at this sir and I knew you would like it."

It was a botanical calendar worth 20 quid. When I looked up, I saw a big smile on his face, and he had dirt all over his cheeks. There were still leaves in his hair from rolling around on the grass.

"You shouldn't have spent all your money on this. Thank you," I said.

"I didn't," he replied and strutted back to his seat like he had just won an award.

It then dawned on me that he hadn't spent any money on it at all. I didn't even have the energy to investigate. I was totally wiped out and happy that I had them all on the train safe and sound. On Monday quite a few of them had written and illustrated lovely recounts of their trip to Kew Gardens. I was pleased because I spent the whole weekend worrying that it was a complete disaster. I also took Hannah aside and told her that she shouldn't have picked the orchid and explained to her why.

She said, "My mother told me the same thing when I gave her hers."

Enough said.

Every year we arrange various themed weeks to focus the children on one subject or social issue. We have Maths Week, Science Week, Anti-bullying week, Sports Week, etc…the weeks are endless. This week is work week. It is my favourite one as I don't have to do anything and for once I get all the credit for organising it. I gave each class £25 and they had one week to plan, budget, and make a product or a service to sell for a profit at our work fair on Friday after school. For the younger ones it was completely teacher led, but for the year 5 and year 6 children it was an opportunity to show their entrepreneurial skills. They completely took over and did it independently.

This year I had a very entertaining experience with the year 5 class. They were ambitious and decided to decorate T-shirts and sell them for a fiver each. However, they didn't budget correctly and by the time they bought the T-shirts they ran out of money for the fabric paint.

I got this letter under my door today:

Dear Mr P,

We are writing to update you on our project for Work Week and ask you for your help. We decided as a class to make original T-shirts with our artwork and sell them at a high price at the work fair. Unfortunately, we didn't budget correctly and now we have run out of money. We would like to ask you for a loan of another £25 to cover the additional costs of buying the fabric paint.

We have been working hard on our designs and think that we could make a lot of money if we finish them. Pleeeeeeeeaaaaaaaase help us!!!!!!! We will be successful with your help!!!!! As you have told us "Dare to win" and we hope you can invest in us.

Sincerely yours,

Year 5

P.S. Please can you let us know today because Ms Davis needs to go and buy the paints for us.

How wonderful. They ran out of money and now I could teach them a lesson. This was turning out to be even more educational than I thought. I went to their class after playtime and asked to speak to them. You could hear a pin drop. I was holding their letter in my hand, so they knew I had come to give them my answer.

"Thank you for your letter year 5. As you can see, I came immediately to respond to you as you requested."

Some of them were nodding in agreement.

"I have taken all your points into consideration and on this occasion, I have decided (slight pause for dramatic effect) to give you an extension on your loan to finish your project."

There was huge applause and celebratory yahoos. I wished I could get them this excited about reading at home. Once they settled down from their jubilant cries I continued:

"However, for my additional investment to be secure I will need to have something as collateral for the extra money I will loan you. Does anyone know what collateral means?"

Nobody answered.

"Well collateral is something that the bank always insists on if it loans extra funding to high-risk clients. You were already given a loan and now you have asked for more. This makes you high risk, so you will have to give me something of yours with the value of £25 to cover my loan in case you can't pay me back. I have spoken to your teacher and she has agreed with me that I will hold on to your remote-controlled racing car and I will return it to you once you have paid me back."

They all looked on in horror as I went to the cupboard and took out their pride and joy that they play with every chance they get. I held it in my hands with a big smile on my face (I was really enjoying this) and asked them if they had any questions.

"What if we don't make the money?" Wesley asked.

"Well then I will keep the car as payment," I said matter-of-factly.

Another hand shot up. "Yes, Margaret what is it?"

Margaret was indignant and I could detect the anger in her voice. "But that car costs more than £25. That's not fair." She was pointing furiously at the car as if to prove its worth.

I continued very business-like. "I know, so I will be selling the car to another class and whatever is left over from the £25 I will give back to you. But I don't think it will be too much because it isn't new, and it has some damage from all the crashes you have had with it."

I smiled and I knew they hated me at this precise moment in time. "Unless there are any other questions (they looked on in horror as I handed Ms Davis the money and walked out with their car. I stopped at the door and turned around) I almost forgot…best of luck."

I was hoping they would rise to the challenge. As I was walking down the stairs, I could hear Ms Davis in her bossy voice trying to motivate them: "Right we don't have much time, so I will send Mrs George to the shop to get the paint and we will start immediately when she gets back. We can do this!"

They didn't do it. They worked their socks off, but the paint was expensive, and they didn't use it sparingly, so they couldn't make enough to cover the loan. However, the T-shirts were works of art. I went back to them to announce the results.

"As you know children you only sold eight T-shirts and at £5 each that makes a grand total of £40. You were given an initial £25 and an additional loan of £25, which makes your total loan that you need to pay back to the school £50. You are £10 short. I will give you 24 hours to come up with a plan to make up this difference otherwise I will sell your car to make back my £10."

Later that day another letter was pushed under my door:

Dear Mr P,

Thank you for this opportunity to earn back our beloved racing car. We know that you are a kind and compassionate person, who always looks out for us and has our best interests at heart, and that is why you have given us this chance. We have come up with a plan that we think will meet with your satisfaction. Ms Davis has helped us come up with this plan and we thank her. Our biggest mistake was buying too many T-shirts and not enough paint. So now we are going to use our sewing skills to make designs on the T-shirts and sell them after school for a reduced price of £2, so we can give you what we owe you. We think this will be successful because it is not costing us anything and we will make them beautiful.

This time I decided to write back to them:

Dear Year 5,

Thank you for your letter and your proposal. I have taken all your points into consideration and I have made the decision to extend the time of your loan for another 4 weeks. Your plan is a good one and it proves that you are willing to compromise, and problem solve.

I wish you the best of luck in your project and look forward to seeing your designs.

Yours sincerely,

Mr P

It only took them a couple of weeks and they managed to sell them all and make a respectable £30. They gave me back my £10 and the other £20 went to the winning pot. We bought some books for the class library. I let them choose. Job well-done and hopefully they will remember this experience as adults when ruthless money lenders and banks keep offering them loans that they can't pay off.

18 November

Today I saw my parent who complained about the Halloween homework. I haven't had a response to my letter, so I decide to approach her and say hello.

She was looking sheepish, and I could tell that she didn't want to have a conversation with me, but I persisted and when I saw she just wanted it all to go away I said, "I'm sorry about that misunderstanding with the homework a few weeks ago. I hope it's all cleared up now."

"I'm sorry too, I was just upset as her father saw it and he was angry," she admitted.

"No need for anyone to be angry. I'm glad we can move on now," I responded with a smile and asked after her two-year-old in the pram. Her face immediately brightened up and we chatted for a bit about preparing her for our nursery in a year's time. This sufficiently distracted her and put an end to this nonsense.

Walking away I felt a bit bad because I was convinced it was her husband who dictated that letter to her, and she was just collateral damage. I wonder if she'd showed him my response.

19 November

David's behaviour has been deteriorating. Almost every day we have an incident in the playground. He was recently diagnosed with autism, and we got him a fantastic 1:1 teaching assistant named Frank to work with him and keep him engaged. He's not too bad in class, but he gets angry very easily when he's playing a game and he's unpredictable. I have tried to keep him occupied with smaller groups during playtimes, but he likes playing with his whole class and he's become popular with the other children. He has a wonderful personality and when he's in a good mood he is delightful. He's funny and kind and when given responsibility he takes his jobs seriously. He's also good with little children, so we get him to mentor the little ones twice a week and this has minimised his outbursts. I try constantly to catch him in a good mood and have a laugh with him, so we can build a relationship. It's important to have credit in the bank with good experiences.

This is his third school and that should have sent some alarm bells ringing at the local authority, but their hands are tied in this insane 'right' for parents to choose whatever school they want. They rarely consider that a pupil with extreme behaviour or special needs is completely disrupted with change, especially if they are on the autistic spectrum. But nobody wants to offend parents' rights as if this will lose them votes down the road somewhere. Bollocks!

Today David had an extra difficult outburst. He finds it impossible to accept losing in a game and blames the other children for cheating. This is not uncommon for most children, but where most of them begrudgingly accept their fate, David just goes nuclear. Today he started by kicking over all the bins in the playground. When the teacher tried to calm him down, he knocked her hand away and locked himself in a cubicle in the toilets. I arrived when he was in the cubicle, so I tried to coax him out.

I said to him, "David, we can't have a conversation in the toilets like this. Come out and we can discuss what happened."

He replied to me, "Why, is it too stinky in here for you? You should make sure it doesn't smell so bad." His response almost made me laugh, but it was a desperate hysterical laugh you get when you are utterly helpless.

With the right training he could someday be a great litigator. He has arguments ready for any topic and coupled with his autism he persistently sticks to points that you can't deviate from. I know when I'm defeated, so I left him with Frank, who managed to convince him to come out.

It took an hour to calm him down, but when we told him that there would be consequences to his behaviour, he turned into what I could only describe as the incredible hulk. He ran out of the school screaming that he was going to kill himself and four of us followed him down the road to ensure his safety. After a thirty-minute standoff in the street he eventually came inside. It was now two hours after the incident began and almost time for him to go home. He had recently acquired permission to go home alone, but we called his older brother to come and collect him. He didn't know this, and we kept it from him until the end of the day because we knew he would not like it. When I told him that he must wait for his brother to come and take him home, he lost the plot completely.

Suffice to say it took five of us taking turns to restrain him, so that he wouldn't run out of the school and possibly hurt himself and others. I was terrified by this point as he was so strong. I could now believe accounts of people lifting cars in total panic. At some point he yanked my arm so hard I thought it had come out of its socket. I let go and the sports coach took over. David was screaming and crying, and the hall was evacuated as I had little children waiting to go to clubs.

This lasted for about five minutes until his brother arrived. He completely calmed down and went with him in a rather docile fashion, which was even more disturbing considering a few seconds earlier he had been screaming bloody murder. Those unexpected mood swings are impossible to manage. I can't predict which strategy is going to work with him and which one is going to completely set him off. Staff are so afraid of his outbursts that they are refusing to work with him. My priority is the child's safety and well-being, but I also have a duty of care to my staff who are entitled to work without feeling such anxiety. Sometimes I'm damned if I do and I'm damned if I don't.

It took another hour to write everything down (another insane but necessary process to have all the evidence in writing) and then I met with all the staff involved to check how they felt and if they had any questions. I always need to ensure that they are looked after as well.

Once all the documents had been completed and social services called and letters posted, my lovely special needs co-ordinator just sat with me in my office to make sure I was okay before I went home. I could feel my heart racing and my hands were a bit unsteady. This didn't happen every day, so it had come as a bit of a shock. I was grateful she took the time to look after me because there was no way I could have gone home and explained to C what kind of day I had had without bursting into tears again. Once the adrenalin had worn off, I realised my right arm was in agony. I forgot about the physical pain.

21 November

David hasn't come to school since the incident. I think his mother is keeping him off on purpose. I guess we just wait for social services to go in and see what happens again. I contacted the Education Welfare Officer to pay them an unannounced home visit. I had covered all the bases and I hoped we could resolve this and get him back on track.

One of my lovely teaching assistants brought me a cupcake today. She bakes party cakes and cupcakes on the side. It is a beautiful cupcake and yummy. She is one of the unsung heroes of the school. She has worked here most of her adult life (thirty years) and has not once lost her sparkle. Her enthusiasm is as infectious today as it probably was thirty years ago. The children love her, the parents adore her, and the staff respect her hard work and dedication. She is the person every parent looks forward to leaving their child with. Thank you, Donna for being so wonderful to so many children. You deserve a damehood.

I ate the cupcake quickly, just to get a good sugar rush, and went off to a meeting about a building project over the summer holidays. We are building a new classroom to accommodate for making our main hall bigger. I don't think the Victorians had so many resources to store in a hall like dining tables, mats for PE, climbing frames, mobile kitchen servers etc. This way we can have events in the hall without cramming people in like cattle.

The meeting was with the architects and the project manager. We discussed the timeframes and went over the preliminary budget. I relied mostly on the experience and knowledge of the experts in the room, but the person who signs the contract and the cheque is me. I needed to understand everything and when they began to talk about the architect's designs, I knew I was struggling. I struggled to imagine a two-dimensional design in a three-dimensional space. I looked at the piece of paper on the table and only saw a box with measurements and lines. I listened attentively as they used jargon I wasn't familiar with and fell deeper and deeper into my imposter syndrome. I was just expected to know the best place for an extractor fan in the toilets and whether two square metres is enough for a reading corner.

I stood up and told them that they had to walk me through the space so I could understand what I was looking at. We went outside and began to walk on the plot of land and almost immediately I could see it all appearing before me. I physically tried to stand in each space and then my teacher instincts kicked in. I noticed that the height of the sinks would be too high for the children. I even went and got the tallest child from that class, and he still couldn't reach the height they used in the plans. This meant that all the measurements were wrong, because they weren't taking the height of the youngest children into consideration.

So now who's the expert? I no longer felt like an imposter today.

22 November

I made a point of standing at the gates this morning to see if David and his mother would come to the meeting we had scheduled. I waited until 9:30, but they didn't show up. As I was about to leave, I saw him running down the street on his own. When he got to the door he was completely out of breath.

I gave him a big smile and said, "I'm so happy to see you. We've all missed you."

"Stop lying, Mr P," he said in between catching his breath.

"I'm not lying, I haven't heard a good joke from anyone in days," I said to him.

He looked up at me and in all seriousness said, "Is that why you're telling me one now?"

I laughed and patted him on the back. "Is your mum coming to the meeting?"

"No, she has to go to work," he said.

"Okay," I said. "You're late so do you want me to take you up to your classroom and tell your teacher you were just talking to me."

He nodded vigorously as he probably didn't want to be told off first thing in the morning.

As we went up the stairs he said, "Knock knock, Mr P."

"Who's there?"

"Hatch."

"Hatch who?"

"God bless you."

I laughed spontaneously. It was funny. I turned around and saw he was laughing too and when he laughed, he tipped his head to one side. We went into the classroom and he sat next to Frank. He gave him a fist bump and I knew today was going to be a good one.

29 November

I had a deputy head teacher shadowing me today as part of her headship course. It's odd having someone following you around all day. Part of me felt on display, which is always disconcerting, and another part of me wanted to show her something useful. I couldn't predict how the day was going to unfold, so I just let it happen. Most of the day was peaceful. She observed my assembly on resilience and commented on how useful it was for her to see how fun they can be. Of course, most adults have terrible memories of dull assemblies where the head teacher just goes on and on without any awareness of the audience. I told her to think of her assemblies as uplifting, one-act plays. The audience should always leave with something new.

We did most of the learning walks in the morning. I showed her how to check for progress in the books and how to canvas pupils effectively on their learning. I asked her to observe a lesson with me and then discussed with her what feedback we should give the teacher. We spent the afternoon going through the school development plan and how to evaluate outcomes. It was almost the end of the day and I was worried that she would leave thinking headship is just so rosy, as the day had happened to be a smooth one.

All of a sudden one of the girls in year 4 came rushing into the reception office and I heard her saying that Daniel had gone 'low', and the teacher had asked for his mother to be called. This worried me because he had recently been diagnosed with diabetes and his sugar levels were all over the place. I explained to my 'shadow' what the situation was and told her we need to go and check that he was okay. He was sitting in the reception office looking very disorientated and confused. His sugar levels had been plummeting quickly these days. The teaching assistant told me that they had checked his levels before PE and he took his insulin as planned, but this was not looking good.

By the time we took out his kit to check his sugar levels again, he started losing consciousness and swiftly started falling off the chair. I grabbed him before he fell to the floor and I put him into the recovery position. We checked his sugar levels and they were not that low, but it was clear that he was crashing fast. I got on the phone to call the ambulance service and they told me it would be at least twenty minutes before they got there. They put me through to 111 and a nurse was talking me through what to do. Daniel's teaching assistant was on the floor next to him checking his breathing. They instructed us to count his breathing out loud so the nurse could hear the counts. The telephone cord wasn't long enough to reach the teaching assistant, so she had to count and I had to stay on the phone for instructions. It was the longest twenty minutes of my life.

When the paramedics arrived they quickly took over and gave him more insulin and he immediately came to. One thing I didn't know was that when people experience a sudden hypo, they can come back very distressed, so Daniel took one look at the paramedics and started screaming. It was scary. I held his hand and told him to look at me and reassured him he would be okay. My familiar face calmed him down and we got him to sit on the chair.

A few minutes later he was laughing and back to his bubbly, normal self. His mother arrived as the paramedics were leaving and we had a chat with her about his insulin and routines. I gave Daniel a head teacher's pencil for being so brave and sent him home a bit early with his mum. It was almost the end of the day anyway. I turned to go to my office and standing there was my 'shadow'. She now looked white as a ghost. I'd forgotten she was there. We went back to my office and continued with the school development plan.

A few minutes later she admitted that she was still a bit shocked at what she had witnessed. I stopped immediately what I was doing. Of course, she was in shock. I explained to her that it was shocking, but over time you realise that as long as they are safe and back at home you have done your job for the day. I reassured her that this was something you learned in time and nobody could teach you. Well, at least my 'shadow' saw a real day.

30 November

Today my deputy head teacher was showing around a group of other deputy heads. They are all on the same course to be head teachers and this module is about school vision. I always struggled with this concept.

They came to my office for a chat and asked me in all seriousness, "What is your vision?" Oh god. I knew it was somewhere written in my school development plan and I saw it every day on my door. I even shared it with my 'shadow' yesterday. I knew it had something to do with excellence and God sprinkled on top, but to the life of me I couldn't remember the exact words. I just looked them all squarely in the face and with all honesty said, "Just work hard and don't mess it up." They laughed and I think they appreciated the honesty. Maybe they also struggled with understanding what a 'vision' was without being a clairvoyant.

My deputy head told me later that they all wrote it down and shared what I had said with everyone on the course at the local authority. Great, I thought. *They already think I'm a loose cannon, now no one will take me seriously. Oh well I have bigger fish to fry with looming cuts in school budgets on the horizon.*

1 December

Christmas play rehearsals have begun in earnest. Let's hope this year the parents don't get into a fight at the Christmas show. Last year I had to stop the play when two parents got into a massive row in the back of the auditorium because they were getting in each other's way of filming the play on their massive iPads.

I say at the start of the performance every year, "Please switch off your mobile phones, don't share any photos on social media of other people's children and you don't need to film it because we are doing it for you. Just sit back and enjoy."

Do they listen? Hell no.

They continue to film it, even on their little phones and spoil their own experience by watching the whole thing through a small screen when they have a spectacular live view of real people right in front of them.

Last year they were particularly belligerent, and fearing the row could become physical I had to make my way on stage, stop the play and reprimand them like children.

I announced rather annoyed, "You are being unfair to your own children who have worked so hard to prepare this play for you. Now put all your phones and iPads away and just watch the show." I then turned to the children and said, "I'm sorry children, but sometimes we adults can be reeeeeaaaaally silly."

The children laughed and I was hoping the parents got the message and felt embarrassed for their asinine behaviour. The play finished without any more dramas, although you still had people's phones ringing during the performance, and they had the audacity to answer the calls. They left a heap of rubbish on the hall floor as if they had gone to the cinema and the staff and I then spent another hour after school cleaning up after them. A few parents stayed behind to help, but the majority cleared off.

The best Christmas anecdote I've ever heard came from another head I know. Her school was in a similarly challenging area as mine and was a church school as well. At one of the Christmas Nativity Plays (which are always nativities or some variation of the story) one parent yelled out in the auditorium, "Oi Mrs Richardson, why this fucking story again?" No words.

However, the thing I can't stand in the run up to Christmas is the amount of glitter everywhere. It is the devil's stardust sent to insidiously permeate every corner of my being. The classrooms are full of it as they make their cards for their families and of course their beloved head teacher. They use the most glitter for the cards they make for me. They are dripping in it. Even the envelopes are completely laced in this poison. I read the cards and of course must display them in my office so I don't hurt anyone's feelings, and those shiny little pieces of evil end up everywhere and I mean everywhere: on my clothes, on my face (most embarrassing when I'm in a meeting and another head teacher comments on the lovely shade of sparkle on my eyes).

I once tried to ban it in school, but the teachers were horrified at the idea of not having their sparkle for the special occasions. Most importantly it's bad for the environment. I thought it would be a no brainer. But they insisted and I was not going to win this one, so here we go: another year of Lucifer's elixir sent to drive me crazy.

2 December

I am getting on my soap box today to play the role of angry citizen. I'm sick to death of people using the word 'bullying' out of context. Every bit of disagreement, conflict, difference of opinion or even argument has become bullying. Parents and children are being sold a cock and bull story by the media that every time they have a conflict, they can define it as bullying and demand that schools deal with it in this vain. I blame the media completely for the misuse of this term and they need to be held accountable for the disservice they have done to society with the misappropriation of the word.

Conflict in school is a very necessary part of growing up. It is a sign of a successful school when children are equipped with the necessary skills to deal with any conflict that comes their way. But to name every bit of conflict immediately as bullying is harmful to those people who are genuinely being bullied.

Today I had a parent and child in my office screaming bloody murder about an isolated incident that the mother was claiming was bullying. Her daughter was hurt by one of her classmates while they were playing hide and seek. Instead of tagging her, he pulled her by her coat and tore it. It was a genuine accident. However, the mother has complained about this child before and keeps focussing on the fact that he's got special needs. The child is autistic, though the incident has nothing to do with his autism. It could have happened to any child regardless of need. It was in no way malicious. Nor was it bullying. But in their very 'narrow' understanding of human behaviour some parents immediately go for the easy option and try to define situations with terms that get the maximum effect. This is how they get everyone's attention.

"What are you going to do about this bullying," she said emphatically.

"Well, firstly this isn't bullying. It was an accident," I replied.

She got angry when I said that, and I could tell she was ready to lose it.

She raised her voice. "Well this isn't the first time and I want him separated from her."

I asked her daughter if they play together and she said that they were friends. The little girl even said that she understood that he has special needs and sometimes makes mistakes. So, I focused on the child because they are so much easier to reason with than most adults. Go figure.

"Lucy, do you think that Evan is trying to hurt you on purpose?" I asked.

"No, he doesn't mean it," she replied immediately.

Here we go from the mouths of babes.

However, the mum chimed in now even angrier that I got the truth from her daughter and continued with this ridiculous bullying explanation. "If this bullying doesn't stop her father is going to come in and sort you lot out."

"And what will her father do to sort us lot out?" I asked matter-of-factly.

She didn't answer and immediately sulked. I was sure she wanted to say that he would come in and beat the shit out of me, but she knew when to stop.

I continued focussing on Lucy. "So why don't we have a plan to help you and Evan when you are playing together. If you notice that he isn't playing nicely or he is too excited, why don't you go and tell an adult and they will come and help. If you don't want to play with him then we can sort that out too. It's up to you, Lucy. Do you want to continue playing with him and help him out when he gets into a muddle?"

Lucy chose to continue playing with Evan and helping him out. Mum rolled her eyes and let out an audible sigh of frustration. I could tell she was not happy that Lucy chose this but didn't say anything about it.

"Well, that's fine, but if he hurts her again then I'll be back," she said.

It was like the terminator "I'll be back…"

"Well let's hope this is the last time. But remember accidents happen all the time," I responded.

I don't think we resolved anything. I just bought some more time to see if Lucy could learn that Evan is different and needs a different approach. The unfortunate thing is that the mum needs to have her insecurities fed and her daughter knows how to do that and get the maximum attention. She knows exactly which buttons to press.

That evening I sent the following letter home to the whole school:

Dear Parents and Carers,

I would like to take this opportunity to address a rather serious issue with you. It has come to my attention that schools, the media, and families have a different working definition of the term bullying. I would like to share with you the definition the school and staff use to determine if a situation is considered bullying. This is from the national centre against bullying:

Bullying: The definition of bullying is when an individual or a group of people with more power, repeatedly and intentionally cause hurt or harm to another person or group of people who feel helpless to respond. Bullying can continue over time, is often hidden from adults, and will probably continue if no action is taken. What bullying is not: single episodes of social rejection or dislike, single episode acts of nastiness or spite, random acts of aggression or intimidation, mutual arguments, disagreements, or fights. These actions can cause great distress. However, they do not fit the definition of bullying, and they're not examples of bullying unless someone is deliberately and repeatedly doing them.

I would appreciate it if you shared this information with your children at home as we do in school. It is important to clarify this for yourselves firstly and then to explain it to your children and use it when they might have any conflicts in school.

Although we endeavour to minimise conflicts, we cannot make them disappear. We teach children how to resolve these conflicts in a responsible and reflective manner and indeed how to seek help when necessary.

Everyone deserves a fresh start.

Please join us for our whole school assembly next week, where the children will be performing a play to highlight what bullying is and how to deal with it.

Have a lovely weekend.

Yours Sincerely,

Mr P

Head Teacher

I knew I would pay for this letter on Monday, but I didn't care. Sometimes you just have to say it like it is. I hadn't offended anyone and it's about time we said our peace too. At home I was feeling triumphant and showed C my letter. I got a quizzical look in reply, "Are you sure?" was the response. "Yes!" I said emphatically not so sure I'd done the right thing but having committed myself to the task.

5 December

I went to work expecting a barrage of e-mails from parents complaining about my letter, but nothing. That's a good sign, so I prepared in earnest for my assembly on bullying. I was going to have a couple of my teachers bully me. I was sure the children would love it and I thought maybe some of the staff would secretly relish it too.

I went out into the playground at 8:45 to greet the children and parents. At the gates I asked a couple of parents not to smoke. They were obliging and put out their cigarettes, but I could tell they were not happy with me. As I walked away, I wondered if I had the right to do that. They were going to smoke at home anyway. Who made me policeman of the world? I don't think I will do that again; it is patronising.

I started my assembly today with my laptop connected to the big screen. I opened pretend e-mails from a teacher, who was writing rude things to me. One of the 'e-mails' said, "I don't agree with the way you run the school. The silly rules you are making will never work and I will make sure nobody from the staff follows them. The children call you names behind your back and the parents hate you."

I read the letter to the children and they went wild. They couldn't believe a teacher would write these things to me. It was hilarious how easy it was to send their imaginations spiralling out of control. I showed them that the letters went on for weeks. The teacher tried to get others against me by spreading horrible lies.

After the children (and some of the parents in the audience) had thoroughly enjoyed the 'abuse' I received, we discussed which bits of the comments are considered bullying behaviour. It was good that they could identify that some of the comments were just disagreements and difference of opinion, but they all agreed that the repeated and malicious nature of the messages were abusive and bullying. It was good to see that they were all in agreement that conflict can happen, but it's the intent and frequency that matter.

After the assembly I couldn't help but wonder how systems bully people too. For example, when we have our results printed in league tables and some schools are humiliated year on year isn't that a form of bullying? In a system that quantifies education based on numeric results someone will always be at the top and someone at the bottom. It's the mathematical law. Why should we be named and shamed in the most public of ways? These league tables make or break careers of leaders. I'm sure this repeated and intentional act can be deemed as bullying. But we continue to praise and reward those schools for exceeding the average results (because meeting them is not even enough anymore). We are told to not focus on the learning, but the outcomes of these SATs tests. Consultants come in and make sweeping judgements based solely on these results. Our own earning power and professional trajectory can be determined solely by the success or failure of these tests. If anything should keep me up at night, it should be the welfare of my children and not if we exceed the national average on these SATs tests.

6 December

Being a head teacher has allowed me the opportunity to confront many of my own vulnerabilities. It is through these I have become a stronger, more resilient person. When I see the extent to which many of my children are neglected it breaks my heart. Their natural resilience is miraculous. I have seen children come in day in and day out without breakfast and some without dinner the night before. I have always taken pride in ensuring that the one meal the children get in school is of the best quality we can provide for the money we are given. Without fail I go into the dining hall every day to check the food, sometimes try it, but always ask the children if they enjoyed it and if they had enough. I hope I haven't failed them in this way.

However, what worries me the most is the comparisons that happen between children. For all their compassion and kindness, children can be the harshest, sometimes cruellest of critics.

Boys usually just rubbish each other about their football prowess or trainers. Girls, on the other hand, have the emotional intelligence to conduct a campaign of insidious torture for years on end. Trying to sort out problems with the girls is like walking through a minefield. Even the best trained counter-intelligence operatives would probably find sorting out a conflict between five twelve-year-old girls a stretch too far for their skill set. We once received flyers in our pigeon-holes from MI5 trying to recruit us. I thought this was a joke, but when a colleague and I called to enquire they said that it was a genuine campaign to recruit teachers because we had transferrable skills in dealing with conflict. I guess trying to sort out fights and arguments in the playground between children is a bit like sorting out two petulant world leaders acting like children.

I've recently been trying to get to the bottom of a situation with some of my year 6 girls who have had a massive falling out, which has escalated to some abusive behaviour on social media. The messages have ranged from silly name-calling to some nasty comments about looks and clothes:

"u know u look like the monkey in the London Zoo we visited last week."

"ur mother tries 2 slap the ugly off u."

"Why do u buy all ur clothes at charity shops."

"my older sister is going to get u!"

"Watch ur back after skool."

The messages went on for weeks. Luckily, the parents all agreed to take away their phones until we sort it out. Maybe this wouldn't have happened in the first place if they didn't give them phones at the age of twelve.

We have been meeting once a week for the past five weeks to get to grips with the situation and try to resolve their problems. I still can't get to the core of the issue. They bring up things that happened in Reception class and that was almost seven years ago when they were just five. How can that be possible? Today we had another summit. From what I gathered there had been a power struggle between the queen bee, Ola, and another up-and-coming leader, Maya.

Well, it's about time they dethrone Ola, I thought. *She's been ruling them with an iron fist since Reception class and now they are revolting.* I was getting sucked into it but it's compelling sometimes.

So, the up-and-coming queen bee has forced some shifts in allegiance and is marginalising the original 'queen bee'. This is a bit like *Game of Thrones.* She has left her with just two followers, and I could tell their allegiance was flailing. This was bound to happen, but I was hoping it would happen in Secondary School and I would miss the drama. Today's topic of conversation was showing empathy.

The new 'queen bee', Maya, volunteered first. "When no one wanted to play Ola's game because it was boring, I let her join in with my game. I showed her empathy." She had a very nasty smile on her face when she finished speaking and sat up straighter on her imaginary throne.

Wow, she has just slapped her in the face with this backhanded empathy malarkey, I thought.

But I persisted trying to break through. I asked Ola how that made her feel and whether she thought that showed her empathy. Ola looked miserable. She was not used to having her games rejected. From a young age she was precocious and managed to attract all the attention of the girls. She is the most clever and imaginative of the lot, but very bossy and I can see why the others got tired of this. Maya is very street smart and although all these years she has

145

been under Ola's spell, she has acquired confidence and began her challenge to usurp the crown.

Ola was nearly in tears. She told Maya that this wasn't kind because she told all the others not to play her game because it was boring.

"Oh dear," I said. "This isn't showing empathy for how she is feeling. Maya, you shouldn't have rubbished her game," I said emphatically.

"Well, she's been rubbishing our games since Reception class, so now she has empathy, because she knows how it feels." She cocked her head to one side and smiled that broad smile of triumphant victory as she readjusted her newly acquired crown.

"Making someone feel just as bad as you did isn't empathy, but revenge," I said, "and this disappoints me, Maya. I thought you were kinder than that."

She just rolled her eyes at me and dismissed my comment. I even thought I heard her kiss her teeth at me, but I let it go. Any more questioning and I may soon become the target of her campaign to rule the world. I was slightly fascinated and scared at the same time.

I brought the others into the fray to see what they thought and hopefully put Maya down a peg or two. I directed my attentions to Maya's second in command. Let's see how loyal she was to her new queen.

"So, Bianca, I thought you and Ola were friends all these years. I remember when you won the talent show with your dance routine." I enquired in all innocence, however, the second I mentioned the talent show I could see the others throwing looks at each other and I could swear they were having a telepathic conversation.

What have I done? I thought. *You should have known better than to bring up the talent show. Don't you remember the drama of who was going to be in it, what song they were going to use, what they were going to wear etc, and not to mention the tears and tantrums when one of them was sick on the day and couldn't make it.*

I had stupidly just opened a Pandora's Box.

I got nowhere today apart from confirming that the rude comments on messenger had stopped. By the time they left I was relieved to find two boys waiting outside my office.

"What happened with you two?" I asked.

"We got into a fight over the football and Mr Riley sent us to you," one of them said.

"Whose fault was it?" I asked.

Edward chimed in first and said, "Well I tackled him, and he fell down. Then he got angry and kicked me." He was rubbing his leg to show me the extent of the pain. It was obviously an act.

"Were you going for the ball or his foot?" I asked.

"The ball," he said emphatically lying to my face.

"Are you both okay?" I asked.

They quickly nodded in agreement.

"Have you apologised to each other?" I continued.

They immediately said sorry and shook hands.

"What's your punishment?" I enquired.

They both replied in unison, "We miss a football session this week."

"That's right," I said. "Now go back and apologise to Mr Riley for having been so silly."

Later that afternoon they were playing table tennis together. They didn't even see me checking up on them. All had been forgotten.

I also went out so I could check up on the girls. They were still in their respective camps, but when they saw me, they scurried to join forces in a show of solidarity or maybe a truce. I watched them watching me for about ten minutes. I went to my secret viewing spot up on the third floor and by the time I got there, they were on opposite sides of the playground once again. I think next week I will have the deputy have a crack at them. I give up.

7 December

If I hear one more Christmas carol, I'm going to scream! My office is right behind a classroom and any free minute the teacher has is spent on practising for the Christmas play. The only thing that keeps me sane is that it will never be as bad as the time *Frozen* hit our screens. The song "Let it Go" will be etched in my memory forever. At one point the children would sing it every day before lunch and at home time, just in case I didn't catch the morning performance; I was sure not to miss the matinee. I even found myself humming it one evening and C looked at me and just burst out laughing.

"Why are you laughing at me?" I was perplexed.

"Do you realise you've been humming the theme tune from *Frozen* all night."

I laughed too. "For the love of God, I need to get them hooked on another film."

I love everything about Christmas but working in a school has made it exceedingly difficult to sustain enthusiasm for this blessed event. Being a church school adds another level of anxiety to strike the right balance between the religious and the utter nonsense of consumerism.

A child told me the other day that they put up three Christmas trees in his house; one in the living room, one in the dining room

149

and one in his bedroom. Families are borrowing money to buy presents at Christmas. That cannot be right. The same boy with the three trees told me that he gets at least ten presents under each one. I asked him what kind of presents thinking they were little trinkets or novelty gifts, but no, it was an Xbox, new trainers, and a phone.

We are truly living in a disposable culture. I had a lot of things growing up too, but never to the extent that these children have. I remember how long I had my first ever Walkman in the eighties. It was the one with the bright orange foamy headphones. I could play all my mixtapes on it and listen to the radio. I looked after that Walkman better than anything. I think I still have it somewhere in the loft. It might be worth something on eBay as a vintage piece.

I know some schools ask children to bring in their own pencils and pens to save money. I tried this once, by giving them the option to bring in their own equipment, but very quickly the tables were covered in massive pencil cases. They were trying to outdo each other with who would have the fanciest equipment. I was observing a lesson in year 5 one day and they were so distracted by fiddling with their mammoth pencil cases that they got little work done. Not to mention the temptation for theft. The number of times I had to deal with missing gel pens was becoming distracting. I quickly abandoned that project and banned the pencil cases.

"Mr P," two children distracted me from my musings on whether or not I should issue ration cards and start recreating a forties austerity. "My teacher sent me to tell you that there's no heating in our building."

"Why didn't she send you to the caretaker," I said.

"She did but we can't find him," they said in unison.

No surprise there, I thought. "Thank you for telling me."

On the coldest day of the year the heating would conk out. I went into the classrooms to see how cold it was and if we could get through the rest of the day without heating. Thankfully, it wasn't too bad and two of the classes would be doing PE in the afternoon anyway, so we should get away with it for today.

It was 11 a.m., so that gave me about six working hours to sort out the heating with no caretaker to be seen anywhere. I went in to check it myself, but we had a new digital boiler installed in September and I couldn't just crank it up like I used to do with the old one. This is how engineers now tie you in to even more visits and money spent. I was determined not to let a machine take over, so I treated it like any other piece of technology and just rebooted it. A couple of minutes later all the flashing lights came back and it fired up. I put my middle finger up at it and make a victory noise. I turned around and saw the two boys staring at me in utter surprise at the door.

"Can I help you?" I said, desperately trying to ignore my earlier performance.

"Ms Lyons told us to come and tell you that the caretaker is offsite and won't be back until twelve."

"That's okay. Mr P fixed the boiler and it's back on again. Go tell your teacher it's all fixed now," I said.

When they turned the corner, I could hear them saying, "Did you see what he did?" and squealing with laughter. Oh well, at least they didn't see me kicking the old boiler and calling it a piece of crap.

8 December

I had a complaint today from a parent that doesn't want her son involved in the Christmas play because she says it's inappropriate, so I went to sit in on a rehearsal to see what the problem was. It didn't take me long to pinpoint the problem. The whole play revolved around a jewel heist at Christmas time. The detectives, who were a dafter version of dumb and dumber, were on a quest to apprehend the culprits.

So here we are, two weeks before the Christmas show, in a church school and we have a Christmas play about a bank robbery. Great! What were these teachers thinking? It is the first year I have just let them get on with it and look what happens.

I quickly took my deputy aside and said to her, "Do you not see anything wrong with this play?"

She looked at me surprised and said, "Well it is a bit out there, but we thought we would do something different this year."

"Yes, different is good, but doing a play about breaking most of God's commandments in a church school will not go down well with most of our parents," I replied rather annoyed.

I could just imagine the vicar having an apoplectic seizure as he watched it. Luckily, years ago, I had written a few plays about Scrooge, so I pulled one out and gave it to them. Poor kids, they will have to learn a completely different part in two weeks. I didn't lie to the children; I told them I thought the play was rubbish and I tried to jazz it up and said that I wrote one especially for them. Well, that was a bit of a lie, but all was fair in love and Christmas productions.

Luckily, this year the children who have the main roles were good at learning lines and not just chosen because their parents complained last year that they weren't in anything. I can't believe how difficult it is to get parents to understand that not all children can have main roles. That's not possible.

One of these years I will just have a concert and no shepherds, no angels, no donkeys, and no tea towels.

9 December

It has been so dark today. I don't know how they do it in the Scandinavian countries. The light has disappeared completely. At least we have the holidays to look forward to. I've even started enjoying the Christmas festivities this year. It's a bit like Stockholm syndrome; you begin to accept the torture and even get pleasure out of it.

Today was odd socks day. At least I got to miss the excitement of 'wear your pyjamas to school' day for Children in Need. I made sure I booked myself on a course that day. There's nothing more embarrassing than having to wear your pyjamas to school and then tell children off or sit through a meeting trying to be taken seriously as you look like you've just rolled out of bed. So at least wearing odd socks isn't too bad. I think I've probably done it by mistake on many occasions.

I went out early into the playground with my trousers rolled up to show off my odd fluorescent socks. The children were squealing with laughter at the sight of my hot pink and canary yellow socks. The children donate 50p to charity. It's a minefield to manage all these events. As if we don't have enough on our hands with teaching and learning and getting them through the SATs, we also support social events that their parents should be promoting with them at home. It's easy to dump it all on schools. We have the people; we

155

have the facilities; and most of all we have the good will. What annoys me most is the lack of gratitude for all the extras that my teachers offer without even a thank you. Not only do we not get thanked, but we also get complaints about not doing it right.

Today we took a class to the local cinema to see a film as a treat for Christmas. We hardly ever recoup all the money that it costs to take children on trips and only ask the parents for a nominal contribution of a couple of pounds for any trip that is not part of the curriculum, i.e., museums or learning centres. On most occasions the cinema will throw in popcorn and a drink with the tickets, but it wasn't offered to us this time.

When they got back at the end of the day, I was dealing with a serious incident where a parent who didn't speak a word of English got separated from her daughter on the road and we were trying to find her.

I was on the phone to the police, when one of the parents whose children went to the cinema came to complain to me that we didn't give them popcorn and a drink.

Are you kidding me? I thought. I just put my hand up and said, "I can't deal with this right now, please go and speak to the teacher."

All hell broke loose. She started screaming in my face and gesticulating to others to get an audience.

"Look at him. He won't even speak to me because he's too busy on the phone. Is this how you treat your parents? You're a joker, you don't care that these children were out all afternoon and weren't given a treat," she ranted. She also threw in that this was a safeguarding issue because that's what they have learned has maximum effect. Last time I checked, not getting popcorn does not constitute a breach in safety or well-being.

I walked away from her because I could feel myself getting angry.

She continued her belligerent rant. "Go on walk away now. Look at him! He's walking away from me because he doesn't want to deal with my complaint." She was throwing her arms in the air like a flapping chicken looking around for others to support her demented rant.

I could hear her voice even when I was on the other side of the school.

Luckily, by the time I got outside to check on the missing girl, she had been reunited with her mother. I was so relieved. There's nothing worse than a child going missing. I then remembered that witch ranting on the other side of the school and raced back to give her a piece of my mind. I was so angry I could hear my heart beating in my head. I was seeing red!

Luckily for me she had buggered off by that point. I would have let it rip if she were there.

The funny thing is that she is a professional woman who works with vulnerable people. Go figure. Some people really don't practise what they preach.

11 December

In all my years as an educator I have thankfully only seen two children that were utterly consumed with rage. David and Ryan. I can still hear the voices in my head taunting me like a horror film. I'll save Ryan for another day because he stayed with us for seven years.

David is a very likable young man. He has a great sense of humour and an infectious laugh. We have managed to keep him on track after what seemed like a disastrous start. However, his mother is one of the most difficult parents to communicate with and I can see how she has sabotaged all the relationships with the other schools and professionals.

To begin with she never answers her phone. This is common practice for parents who have difficult children. They don't really want to deal with it, so they deliberately slow down the process by ignoring all the communication. Some parents have the spectacular audacity to come back and blame the school and the hardworking staff that have been nothing but kind and caring.

David has finally been diagnosed with Autism, ADHD, and emotional dysregulation (a description for people who suffer from extreme mood swings and cannot react calmly to any provocation). This is all an explosive combination. We can never predict what is going to set him off. What we know is that we have a child who is potentially dangerous to himself and others. David is known to terrorise the whole family when he has one of his outbursts and now his behaviour has begun to deteriorate quickly. He had been threatening to kill himself again, so we contacted social services, but they closed the case within a couple of weeks. He has good days and bad, but he's generally an extremely volatile young man.

13 December

Teacher recruitment is getting worse and worse. It is estimated that almost a third of newly qualified teachers quit the state sector within five years. Is nobody listening to these staggering statistics? Yet we plough on with reform after reform of meaningless change that is adding no value to children's learning. Schools need good teachers. Invest in people not white papers.

So here I am trying to find a good teacher to cover the maternity leave in February. I've put an advert in the TES which has cost the school a fortune and only had responses from Supply Agencies looking to get a fee if they place someone with us. So now, a bit like the entertainment industry, we go through these pariahs to find a teacher. There should be regulations to prevent this from happening or at least a state sponsored agency to rival these leeches.

Today I observed a candidate for fifteen minutes and thought, *This is rubbish she can't even finish the hour.* After her ten-minute introduction she said to a class of thirty children, who were all sitting on the carpet, "Okay class go and get your whiteboards and pens and come back to the carpet."

It was like watching a car crash in slow motion. There was absolute mayhem with children running to get the boards, arguing over what colour pens they had and some even crawling under tables to get at the cupboard. On what planet do you give an instruction for thirty people to go to one cupboard all at the same time to get equipment? Even if you aren't a teacher your common sense would kick in. Thankfully, the teaching assistant intervened and there wasn't absolute carnage.

The straw that broke the camel's back, came five minutes later when she couldn't access her PowerPoint presentation on her USB stick. She just looked at me and said, "What am I supposed to do now?"

I got up and escorted her out of the classroom and said to her, "You know this isn't going to work out, so thank you for coming in today," and I promptly showed her the door. Oh my god! This does not look good. The search continues. If I don't find someone by February, then my deputy head goes back into class full-time and I will have to pick up the pieces. The children come first.

If worst comes to worst then I will even teach them. The one thing I can guarantee is that I can teach and as a head teacher I'm not afraid of it. It's a bit like being a top surgeon and not performing any operations. You need to lead by example.

14 December

The holidays are coming…the holidays are coming. I put my tree up yesterday and it looks beautiful. I love sitting in the dark room enjoying the twinkling lights. It's magical, and I am like a kid in a candy store when it comes to Christmas decorations. Last year I went to Strasbourg to visit some friends and I came back with a suitcase full of Christmas ornaments for the tree and the house. The experience is like walking into a Christmas card.

It snowed last night, and I can't believe how chaotic it is everywhere. The amount of snowfall is laughable – about 3 inches and everyone looks for a chance to stay at home. I'm sure the North Americans would laugh at us if they saw what constitutes a reason to close a school down. I've never closed the school for snow and told all the staff that if the trains and tubes are running then I expect them to come into work. "I can't drive in," is not a good enough excuse to close a school down and inconvenience all these parents. I'm very unpopular on these days.

I went in super early to make sure I set the example. It's lovely outside. The playgrounds looked amazing, and what I like most about the snow is how muffled everything sounds. There's a soft silence that comes with the snow and I stood outside for a few minutes to enjoy the peace. This might be the calm before the storm.

It didn't last long when the children came in and transformed the white blanket into dirty slush. The caretaker had called in sick. He said he had a bad back. So that left me with a couple of teaching assistants to help me grit the grounds. That's the only nightmare I have. You don't want anyone slipping and injuring themselves because you know they will sue the school. Unfortunately, a very precious mum took a tumble bringing her daughter in late. She's late every day and runs in heels – a bad choice of footwear on this day.

I offered her assistance, asked if she was okay and filled in an accident report once she had left, just in case she was the one that would sue us today. By this point it was 10 a.m. and I hadn't even started on what one would consider work. I had shovelled snow, sprinkled grit all over the playgrounds and tried to make sure the grounds were as safe as they could be. It's these holes you need to plug daily that make you feel like you're on a sinking ship sometimes.

I was determined to enjoy the snow, so I told the teachers to send me two children from each class in the afternoon to build a snowman. We got some old forgotten clothes from the lost and found and dressed them with hats and scarves. They looked wonderful. We took pictures and put them on the website. At the end of the day a little girl in year 2, who helped with the snow couple, brought me a letter. It said:

To Mr P,

Thank you for piking me to make the SNOW MAN! It was the best day for me. I never made a snowman and now i no how to do it proprely. I drawed this for you. It was my best day. Thank you. You are the bestest headteacher in the world.

From Chiara

There was a brilliant drawing of the snow couple, and she had extended the family with a couple of snow children too. Priceless! I pinned it on my board of children's work in my office.

15 December

It's the Christmas lunch today. Oh the joys of this festive season. Last year the chef got it completely wrong and we ran out of food. I had to run to Tesco and buy as many ready-cooked chicken drumsticks as I could get my hands on. I tried to make it special for the children that didn't get the Turkey dinner and buy them loads of special Christmas crackers. I 'dressed' the table with tinsel and decorations and told them that they were selected by their teachers to have a special Christmas lunch with the head teacher and get treated for being so good. It was odd because some of those children were the naughtiest children in the school and they were confused as to this amazing turn of events. But that was the script and I stuck to it.

This year we have a new chef and he's marvellous, so I'm sure it will be fine.

The Christmas lunch is a big deal as we invite the families to come and join us. This can be a logistical nightmare to manage, but generally it's a fun event. However, this year it is spoiled for me when one parent said to me, "This is worse than a soup kitchen."

"It's not, ungrateful cow," was what I wanted to say, but instead I said, "I'm sorry you feel that way, how do you think we could improve on your experience?"

She had nothing substantial to add and continued to eat the soup kitchen food of which she was so critical.

I tried desperately to ignore her stupid comment and continued to do the rounds around the tables with my silly Santa hat on asking the ones that matter – the children – what they thought. They all gave me the thumbs up and I couldn't help but smile when I saw how happy they were pulling their crackers and eating their Christmas pudding with ice cream.

I went out into the playground and joined in with the children playing table tennis. I'm rather good at it, but I always let them win. They love beating me at games. It's a badge of honour for them, especially the ones that get into trouble; it's almost as if they get back at me if they win and I know it makes them feel better about our relationship.

As the children were lining up a little girl in year 1 gave me a massive hug and said, "Thank you for the crackers and the lunch."

I put on my best Santa voice and said, "You're most welcome, little girl. I heard you have been good all year. Your teacher is immensely proud of you. I will go and tell Mr P to give you a special prize in assembly this week." I finished off with a big "Ho, Ho, Ho, Merry Christmas everyone!"

As she was going back to her line, I heard her say to her friend, "Mr P thinks he's Santa. He's funny."

17 December

Tonight is the Christmas 'do' with all the staff. I look forward to it every year and feel that it's just an opportunity for all of us to come together and let our hair down. Some let it down more than others, but I always make an early escape so I can avoid seeing any staff falling into complete and utter disrepute. All the teachers would love to see me in a state of complete inebriation, but that never happens. I lead these people and once they have seen you drunk you can never erase that image from their minds. It's a bit like your online footprint. Once it's out there it can never be erased.

On one such occasion a teaching assistant, who was young and naïve, was led astray by some of his more savvy colleagues. I could see it happening in slow motion, like a car crash, and could do nothing about it. The staff were on a mission to get him to come out of his shell. He was the quintessential nerd: all buttoned up and reserved, but rather handsome in that Clark Kent kind of way.

As the night progressed, he became drunker and drunker, and I tried to keep him out of trouble and sat next to him hoping my presence would keep him safe. But I couldn't keep the bottles of wine from coming his way. Towards the end of the night, the music changed, and a belly dancer appeared from nowhere. It was a Turkish restaurant, and this was part of their evening ritual. The dancer stopped at our table and began to gyrate her hips around us, paying much attention to the young man, who became enamoured by her swaying hips and hypnotised by her snake-like movements.

Next thing I knew he was standing up and joining her in a less than rhythmic sway of his own hips, resembling a tugboat on choppy shores. The belly dancer offered him some nipple tassels and he promptly unbuttoned his shirt and stuck them on. The clapping and shouting reached a crescendo and at this point I made a swift exit before I ended up in the photos.

A few weeks later I saw the photos up in the staffroom and swiftly took them down. I left a note on the board which read, "I have the photos of the belly dancing — would the owner of the negatives come and see me please." Later that day, the young man and his colleague came to find me to retrieve the photos. They both looked sheepish and couldn't make eye contact. I gave him the photos and said, "Next time eat something before you drink so much. And make sure they don't end up on social media." They laughed a bit and apologised again. No serious harm done.

20 December

It's the last week. Thank God not a full one, but it's going to be busy. The Christmas play is tomorrow and then our church service (another round of carols and presentations) and then we finish with just a couple of days to get our personal Christmas shopping done. My wish is that one year we don't buy each other anything, but just do some good deeds. I try to pass this message on to the children and of course being a church school, we have ample opportunity to discuss the 'real' meaning of Christmas.

But when I look back to my own youth it was the same. All I was concerned with were the presents, and the bigger and more technologically advanced the better. I remember my brother and I were the first kids in the neighbourhood to have the 'Atari' and all the other kids would come to our house to play 'Space Invaders' and my absolute favourite 'Pac-Man'. I still learned the value of Christmas and know how to be giving and loving towards others. All we need is a healthy balance between the old and the new.

Still, it horrifies me to see how far down the technological rabbit hole some schools have gone. At least every couple of weeks I purposely switch off the server at school and then do a learning walk to see how the teachers are coping. I know it's evil, but I can't resist. It's interesting to see how much we are relying on the Interactive

White Boards and the internet to teach. The sign of a great teacher is the ability to adapt and think on your toes.

Those schools that are now buying into the philosophy of computers and smart technology being a substitute for direct human instruction, I think will find themselves at a saturation point. The children will inevitably seek those human contacts and will not have the skills or the emotional intelligence to form them.

I visited a school recently with such an ethos; every pupil had an iPad to communicate with the teacher who sat behind a desk answering their questions. There were no trees in the playground. The outdoor surfaces were all made from artificial soft play material and it made me feel like these children were in a laboratory. On my way out the Business Manager, who had showed me around, declared, "As you can see, we are a school that is connected," and she used the air quotes for the word connected. It seemed more to me like they were so connected that they were disconnected.

It was like last Saturday when I went to my usual cafe after my run to get my cappuccino and their Wi-Fi had gone down and they were only able to accept cash. It was hipster carnage. Nobody in this long queue had any cash on them (apart from me). I sauntered rather triumphantly to the front of the queue picking up all the fallen jaws of the bearded and unwashed hipsters and declared, "Keep it under your mattresses guys, the machines will fail. Viva la revolution." They were not amused. My lovely barista laughed and that's all that mattered.

21 December

I went to the hall this afternoon to help set up for the Christmas plays. We have a tight turnaround from clearing the hall from lunch and transforming it into a Christmas wonderland. Luckily, my lovely parent governors came in early to help. They are so amazing and fully committed to the life of the school. Having them here reminds me how lucky we are to have such a strong community of people dedicated to do the best for our children.

The rehearsals have gone well and even though I changed their play two weeks ago, it's all going swimmingly. Once all the parents had settled in their seats, I introduced the play and pleaded with them to switch their phones to silent and suggested they put everything away and just enjoy the children's wonderful performances. When I finished my speech, they all whipped out their iPad and phones. It was like I was never there.

I was so proud of our little stars. They'd learned their lines in just two weeks and the teachers prepared them well. Apart from a little boy in Reception class who wet himself on stage, it all went off without a hitch. We even got away without having to see any tea towels on children's heads. Hooray.

One more day to go…

22 December

Today we lit our last advent candle in our church service. The children sang carols, and I did a talk on St. Nicholas and St. Basil. Before Santa and his elves were hijacked by the multinationals, gift-giving was a more altruistic experience. So today I reminded everyone that this time of year should be rooted in deep compassion for our fellow people. I drew comparisons of the two saints, showed them icons of their dress which were reminiscent of Santa Claus and shared some of their more popular life stories.

As we break up for Christmas, I feel exhausted. I'm surrounded by way more chocolate than my waistline can manage and more glitter than I can possibly stand. I stayed super late in school on the last day to make sure I had everything ready for our return. It also gave me an opportunity to walk around the school and just get a feel for what was happening in the classrooms. I looked at the children's books and checked on their progress again. We do this officially every few weeks, but I just like getting a feel for it myself.

In year 4 they have been learning about jobs in the community (local heroes) that help us like nurses, police officers, and teachers. One of the children had written a lovely piece about Karen, one of our teaching assistants. She said, "Karen works in my school and looks after me. She is kind and caring and always picks me to help her with the summer fair. When I was upset Karen gave me a cuddle and told me everything will be alright. She sorts out our problems and she makes me laugh. I think Karen is a local hero because she never gives up on us and even when we are naughty, she gives us a second chance. I love Karen."

It all looked good. I felt proud. I left with a spring in my step and a mental note to share this with Karen.

24 December

I was having a lovely lunch with a friend today who was visiting from Cambridge. I was just about to tuck into my duck terrine when I got a call from the electrician at school to say that there was a flood in one of the classrooms. His description was quite graphic, and I thought he might have been exaggerating. I left my friend to finish her lunch on her own.

On my way out she said to me in all innocence, "Shouldn't the caretaker or someone else deal with this? Is it your job too?"

"My dear it is all my job." I gave her a kiss and wished her a Merry Christmas.

In the cab I was thinking how utterly ridiculous this was. It was my holiday and here I was going into school to sort out a flood. I guess it's just like running any business, the buck stops with you. It's not so much about the time invested, but the efforts to try and solve problems you're not even qualified to deal with. It's like giving a plumber a scalpel and asking him to remove a kidney.

The electrician was not exaggerating. The radiator had burst and there was boiling water pumping into the room like a geyser. Even the children's books were dripping wet from the steam. It was like walking into a sauna. On the way to school, I called one of my teaching assistants, Karen, who lived around the corner and thankfully she had come in to help. We ripped everything out and moved as much furniture as we could into the playground to dry.

I was now starting to wonder if we would be able to use the classroom in January. I arranged for the plumber to come in and fix the leak, however, he couldn't come in until the twenty-seventh and it was freezing every night. Without the heating, the pipes could freeze up and burst. Anything else to worry about? The condensation in the room needed more than just airing out. It was just me and Karen; the dynamic duo left to fend for ourselves. It wasn't the first time she had bailed me out of a jam, and I owed her a huge debt of gratitude for keeping me sane all these years.

So here we were, midday, Christmas Eve, traipsing down the high street with two de-humidifiers we rented. The water would need to be emptied every day and tomorrow is Christmas and I have eight people coming over for lunch. Thankfully, Karen offered to come in as she would be home alone with her husband. We had to take it in turns for the next two weeks to come in and empty the buckets of water collected (she offered to do more days than me). We then went into town and bought a carpet to lay down temporarily until the new flooring could be put in. I will have to spend the next two weeks re-decorating the classroom with all the displays that can be salvaged and put up some new ones to replace the damaged ones. I won't tell the teacher until the New Year. There is no point in ruining her Christmas too. Teachers have enough on their plate.

On my way home I just felt a bit numb. All I wanted for Christmas was a trouble-free holiday with no disasters at school.

175

9 January

Happy New Year. No children today. My year 1 teacher brought me a large box of chocolates and an even larger bottle of gin to thank me for not ruining her Christmas. Looking on the bright side, she is a terrible hoarder and I think this was a great opportunity to clear the classroom of all the clutter. I think it looks better even though we are still waiting for a new floor to be put in. I have decided that carpets are not the best solution in a classroom.

After lunch I went to the local authority leadership briefing and we were bombarded for two hours with the following headlines. This is not a joke. I have even left some out:

Data Analysis

School Census

School accountability

Baseline Assessments for Reception class

DFE publications

Keeping Children Safe in Education

Curriculum Resources

Apprenticeships

Teachers' Pay and Conditions

Attendance

Data Protection Toolkit

Staff and Employment Advice

Parental Responsibility

Relationships and Sex Education

Gender Separation in Mixed Schools

Information Sharing

Winter-Readiness

Arts in Schools

ASP (analyse school performance)

School Inspection handbook

British Values

School inspection update (they're coming they're coming they're coming)

PAC and Ofsted (I think PAC is Parliamentary something committee, but will have to look it up as I'm losing the will to live)

Religious Education

PAL (Physically Active Learning)

EFA (Embedding Formative Assessment- a new term to me)

Setting and Mixed Ability

Forgotten Children (I have forgotten my own name by this point)

Using Data to Prevent Bullying

Hierarchy Markets and Networks (WTF!!!!)

Special Needs

Digital Awareness

SEND Governance Review

School Leadership

School Workforce

Schools' Funding

Deals For Schools

School Workforce Planning

Improving Outcomes for Black Children

AND FINALLY, YOU'VE GOT TO BE KIDDING ME:
Staff Well-Being!

What about my well-being for having to sit through two hours of being inundated with all this information, which was making me feel like a complete failure? How on Earth can anyone expect us to absorb all of this? Presenting it to us all in one go is a bit like waterboarding.

Thanks everyone and happy New Year to you too!

10 January

I feel overwhelmed by yesterday's onslaught of information. I can't help but wonder how on Earth we are to sustain this high level of demand and increasing accountability. What worries me most is that the people who are on the receiving end of these endless initiatives are so tired and despondent that they lack any chutzpah to say enough is enough. These are the government's exact words in a report on teacher recruitment and retention:

A key driver for teachers considering leaving the profession is unmanageable workload. The Government and Ofsted must do more to encourage good practice in schools and recognise that changes to the school system and accountability play an important part in increasing workload.

By the time I got to school I felt like the weight of the world was on my shoulders. The school secretary had already texted me to say that she was stuck in traffic, so I made sure any absences were covered. Luckily, everyone was in, so I just needed to manage the buzzer.

I made my way into the playground to see the children. I can guarantee they will lift my mood and distract me. A little boy came running up to me and gave me a massive hug and said, "I missed you so much, Mr P." Once the others saw him, they came charging up to me to wish me a happy new year and by magic my spirits were lifted, my hopes renewed, and my energy recharged. Thank you, children.

I had an assembly today about Epiphany and shared the story of Jesus's baptism. I tried to frame it in a discussion on hope and New Year's resolutions.

The first question I got from one little boy was, "Did Jesus have his clothes on when he was baptised?"

"I'm sure he had a cloth covering his body," I replied, and the room was already full of laughter and sniggering.

He persisted, "I was naked when I was baptised, and you could see my willy."

This was enough for me to lose the room. I was just upstaged by a precocious seven-year-old. He knew exactly what he was doing.

I gave in to the madness and replied, "Well you were a baby when you were baptised and Jesus was a grown man, so it would have been inappropriate for him to be naked."

He seemed to accept this and refrained from any more comments. Although, the cheeky smile on his face betrayed his intentions. He meant to upstage me. Props to him!

I finished the assembly with, "Let's just put our hands together, close our eyes and say the Lord's Prayer."

Nothing can go wrong there until someone farted and the room descended into chaos. I think I will change my morning assemblies to an hour later. At least by that point they won't be farting up their breakfast. I might just get the occasional tummy rumbling.

12 January

Today I interviewed three prospective teaching candidates for the maternity cover. Let's call them dumb, dumber, and dumbest. The first one showed up twenty minutes late. She didn't call, she didn't seem flustered, and she didn't even apologise. I sent her away immediately. The second one had no clue how children learn and thought that by having a fantastic PowerPoint presentation that the children would, by osmosis, know exactly what to do. I went through the motions and interviewed her. When I asked how she could improve her lesson to get better outcomes it was like I sent her into a hypnotic sleep. I could practically hear the crickets in the background. She was completely clueless. Eventually she said that she would have shown them another video in her presentation. *Great!* I thought. Just take up more of their valuable time by making your presentation even longer. I thanked her for coming and I sighed before she even left the room.

Now the third one was spectacularly stupid. She decided to teach an art lesson and throw in some geography and history for good measure. Not a bad idea. She told the children they would be making Venetian Carnival masks. She seemed relatively prepared with all her materials ready. For a split second I thought this one might have some potential. I straightened up and got ready to observe.

My hopes were dashed very quickly when she told the children that Venetia (she pronounced it Veneshia) is a country in Europe and she proceeded to point to Sardinia on the map. *For the love of God!* I thought. *I'm going to have to stop this lesson.* Luckily, she moved swiftly on to the mask making and the children were happy to decorate them, so I let her continue. I didn't proceed to an interview and then she had the audacity to request through her agency to be paid for a half-day's work. I don't blame her, I blame those leeches at the agency. They probably told her she could get paid. Thieves!

By this point it was 12:30 and I hadn't even had a coffee or gone to the toilet since I arrived at 7:30. I went to the dinner hall to check on the lunches and ate with the children. I sat with the year 6 children who had those awful candidates today and I asked them what they thought of them.

"They weren't like our teacher," one pupil declared.

"What do you mean?" I asked her.

"Well, the first one didn't really care about the work we were doing and the second one didn't know where Venice was," she said.

"How did you spot that? The map wasn't that big, and you were sitting at the back," I asked.

She looked at me and laughed and some food spluttered out of her mouth. "We all heard you say under your breath, 'That's not Venice that's Sardinia'."

I laughed. I hadn't even realised I'd done that.

"Will one of them be our new teacher?" they asked.

"No!" I said emphatically. "And by the way, Venice is a city in Italy." Just for the record.

13 January

T.S. Eliot said in *The Waste Land*, "April is the cruellest month". I think any teacher would say that January is the cruellest month. It seems like everyone's spirits have been sucked dry and here I am trying to promote our current Christian value of hope. What I would like to say to everyone is *I hope you all snap out of your foul moods and just get over it.* But January is just morose. It comes immediately after all the debauchery of Christmas and the New Year and everyone is skint. Just sprinkle some foul weather on top and you have the perfect recipe for misery.

So here I was today as the head cheerleader trying to motivate everyone to snap out of their funk. Even the children take on their teachers' moods. It's almost a symbiotic existence. I looked out into the crowd and I saw a sea of miserable faces. I decided to scrap my planned assembly and improvise today. I asked them all to stand up and I immediately saw the annoyance on most teachers' faces. I was not popular today.

I announced rather enthusiastically, "Okay everyone I want all of you to stretch your arms up into the air as far as you can go."

I took out a twenty-pound note from my pocket. I now had their attention. Money talks.

"Imagine there is a twenty-pound note dangling from a string above your head. You can't jump but you must stretch as far as you can to get it. The person who I think tries the hardest will win this twenty-pound note to buy games for their class."

Some of them began jumping and now the teachers were really annoyed.

"If you can't get it by reaching up, why don't we try to blow it off the string? Now blow as hard as you can and see if you can get it off."

It was surprising how many of them believed they could blow this imaginary twenty-pound note off its string. The power of the imagination. Once they were all warmed up and more alert, I asked them to sit down. I could see they were ready to listen, and the teachers were sufficiently wound up to forget their misery. They all just collectively hated me.

"So, children, why were your reaching up to grab the twenty-pound note?" I asked.

"Because you asked us to," replied a sarcastic year 6 pupil, and he looked around for validation from his peers. One of them gave him a fist bump and a pat on the back for being a smart ass.

Everyone laughed including the teachers. I ignored them and tried to look unphased.

"Yes, I know, but what was your motivation?" I continued.

"To win the twenty-pound note," said another.

"Yes, that's right," I said, "but you couldn't possibly know who I would award it to and if it would be a fair test."

"We trust you," said another girl from year 6.

"So, all you saw was the twenty-pound note I took out of my pocket and to earn it you all agreed to do a series of imaginary tasks to get an imaginary twenty-pound note off an imaginary string dangling over your heads." I paused for a moment of reflection and continued. "What kept you going?"

"The hope of winning," said a little boy in year 3. His hand was still up in the air, even though he didn't wait to be called.

Bingo! I thought.

"Exactly!" I said. "Hope is exactly this. Working towards something that you can't really see and you're not even sure is there. You keep going; being positive you will succeed. Hope is not a passive activity. You can't just sit back like a wish and expect it to just happen. Hope needs hard work, positivity and believing in yourself."

I could see I had them now as every face in the room was looking attentively my way. "So, when I say I hope you all do well in your SATs tests I know that your teachers have worked ridiculously hard to prepare you. I know that you have improved your skills. I know that I have checked the progress in your books. Hope isn't a coincidence. It doesn't come by magic. You need to work hard and make it happen."

A little hand went up immediately when I finished.

"Yes Emmanuel," I said.

"What if you fail?" Emanuel said meekly.

"Well then Emmanuel you rely on hope's cousins, resilience and endurance, to see you through until you hope again," I declared pointing at the values on the wall.

He seemed satisfied with that answer and, luckily, we spent last half-term talking about endurance, so it was fresh in everyone's mind. By this point even the teachers seemed more alive. More hopeful I dare say. Sometimes it pays to go off task.

I felt satisfied that I had managed to snap everyone out of their January blues. However, after school at my weekly staff briefing my own words were thrown back at me in utter disdain when a member of staff replied to one of my questions, "I will work harder to get it in on time next term and I hope everyone will help me."

I replied as sarcastically as I could, "Hope is one thing; a miracle is completely different," and I finished with a wicked smile. Message received. The January blues is no excuse for being a smart ass.

16 January

I had a call this morning from social services asking about a family. The children are no longer in my school, but the call did not surprise me. They were all challenging children for one reason or another, but the youngest was the most challenging child I have ever met in my thirty years as an educator. The mother was mostly on her own and she was fiercely religious. The father came in and out of the picture and you could usually tell when he was around because the children's behaviour seemed to deteriorate exponentially during one of his visits. He only stayed long enough to get the mum pregnant and then go off again. I had my suspicions that he had a second family abroad. This little man was a complete tyrant. He terrorised the mother and the children and even tried to intimidate me one day after one of my assemblies.

We had invited the parents to a special assembly where the children were performing Caribbean rhymes using skipping games. We even had Boney M. blaring in the background. At the end of the assembly this man came up to me and introduced himself as the children's father. He needn't have done that as the children were the spitting image of him. He asked after the music I was playing, and I happily showed him the CD, thinking it is a genuine request. He proceeded to accuse me of preaching about Seventh Day Adventism and told me that he will report me to the governors of the school. Knowing a little bit about this bully, I refrained from blowing my top and calmly asked him if he heard me using the words 'Seventh Day Adventism' during my assembly. I reminded him that before he answered this question that I had three hundred people in the hall as my witnesses. He looked me straight in the eyes and said, "Yes I heard you use those words and talk about their beliefs."

Now was the right time to blow my top. I do not negotiate with terrorists, nor do I entertain fantasists like this little twerp. He was not expecting my reaction. Little did he know that he had just pissed off the American immigrant side of me and that man doesn't take any prisoners.

"Get out now!" I commanded rather forcefully, and I pointed to the door.

He was stunned and didn't move, and I know it was more out of sheer horror that I dared to confront him on his own terms. I think he was expecting a white Anglo-Saxon response along the lines of, "Well sir I am sorry you feel this way, but at no point did I preach, as you claim, about Seventh Day Adventism. I am confident that you will not find anyone in the room of three hundred people that will corroborate your claims. Have a good day." And then I should walk away with my head held up high.

No. It did not go down that way. I pointed to the door again; this time I commanded slightly louder, more menacingly and took a couple of steps towards him. "Get out now!" He was off like a shot and luckily not many people around witnessed it, apart from his children. I think they were pleased that someone stood up to him.

His youngest son, Ryan, is a miniature replica. This is the boy that spread fear in our school for seven long years. I even had teachers resigning at the prospect of having to teach him. We had to install extra security gates and change all the release buttons on the gates so he couldn't get out. Ryan was highly intelligent too. This combination is explosive in children who have suffered some type of trauma.

During one Ofsted inspection I had to run down the street chasing Ryan in one of his great escapes. I brought him back kicking and screaming past the window while all three of the inspectors watched during their team meeting about our 'overall effectiveness'. What a sight! At least they couldn't claim I didn't keep him safe. After the inspection, his teacher resigned and the battle to help this child began for a relentless seven years.

Once he realised that he was not going to have his way he terrorised the children and the staff. On one occasion he brought a cricket bat into the classroom and we needed to evacuate. He smashed everything in his power and would not stop. His mother knew how challenging he was and would never pick up her phone. We had to be extra vigilant to catch him out, but his temper always let him down. He had that natural charisma of a tyrannical leader: part charm, part fear.

Ryan was even voted a school councillor; the power of intimidation affecting the democratic process. At first, I thought this responsibility might help to improve our relationship and get him to be a better role model, but he used and abused his power until we had to vote him off the school council.

However, the worst and most disconcerting thing he would do is force himself to cry hysterically to the point where he would hurl and make himself sick. In this state he would scratch his eczema and even make himself bleed. We involved social services over the years, but the cases would be closed almost immediately. I felt sorry for the mother, but she didn't make matters any better as she would go home and just be very punitive or spoil him rotten. These were very conflicting messages.

His older sister said it all one day when she commented on his behaviour at home and said, "It's easier for all of us to do what Ryan wants because then we have a quiet life." I once witnessed his mother having to deal with one of those 'extreme crying' moments in the car when she had to collect him after an exclusion. He was not going without a fight and she had to physically restrain him in the car. Anyone from the outside would have thought this child was being held captive and abused; little did they know he was the one abusing everyone around him. But we persevered for seven years with this young man and kept him in school.

However, it took a toll on the whole school. I think we all suffered a bit from PTSD. He left us five years ago and most of the staff still remember him. Something happens to our faces when his name is mentioned. Whenever we have training on behaviour management or children suffering from mental health problems, his name is the first to come up. The biggest problem with him was that, unlike David, who is a funny and an extremely likable child with a brilliant sense of humour, Ryan was not easy to like. He was downright mean and nasty to everyone. This is a testament to the kindness of my staff who managed to always care for a child we all found difficult to like.

Don't be shocked, it does happen. We are human after all. Therefore, teachers need to be good actors sometimes.

So, as I sat there speaking to the social worker on the phone, I didn't ask her what had happened as I didn't really want to know. I explained to her that these children left us long ago and we do not have any recent information to share. You sometimes need to just draw a very definitive line under it all. I think I'm still traumatised.

18 January

I have four members of staff off sick today. Fantastic way to start the day. My deputy can teach one of the classes. I could only get two supply teachers at such short notice, so I needed to teach the last one. I got the secretary to reschedule a meeting with a parent and I scrambled to find all the lesson plans for four classes. Year 4 had PE today and I was wearing my leather loafers. I was not destroying another pair of shoes. I thought we would just have an extended art session in the afternoon instead of PE. Children never get enough art anyway. It's good for the soul. I cobbled together the lesson plans for the day and went and got the classroom ready.

I went into the playground to collect the children and when they found out I would be their teacher they celebrated and did a lot of fist pumping. That made me happy. I always know I'm doing an okay job if the children still celebrate to be in my company.

By lunchtime I was exhausted (in a good way) and felt happy that I had just spent three hours without answering e-mails, solving anyone's problems, or filling in some stupid pieces of paper. I had taught thirty children how to use a simile in their writing and helped them to understand how to add 4-digit numbers. I didn't have a lunch break because the minute I went into my office to eat my sandwich, I got bombarded by messages from the office.

"Are any of them urgent?" I asked.

"No, but I don't know if I'll see you at the end of the day, so I just wanted to make sure you have them," the admin officer replied. She is superwoman and so efficient and I could never do my job without her.

I hadn't even had a chance to pee since I had arrived at 7 a.m. but I would have to look at these messages and be distracted even further.

No sooner had I had this thought than the phone rang. It was the admin officer who said, "I didn't want to disturb your lunch, but I have the police on the phone, and this is definitely urgent." I took a deep breath, reached over for a piece of paper and pen, and said, "Put them through."

It turned out that one of the parents of a little boy in Reception class had been arrested for shoplifting and they had now discovered that she was an illegal immigrant, so they were not sure if she would be out in time to collect him. They asked if I could keep him in school until they arrived. I told them I can put him in the after-school club and would wait for them to come. It is so difficult for head teachers to commit to anything more regular with the children. You never know when you are going to be pulled away by something 'urgent' and this was 'urgent', unlike the stupid messages from various companies wanting to sell me something.

The afternoon was a disaster as I didn't have time to organise anything. The children had a rotten playtime and lots of arguments spilled into the classroom. I stopped everything at some point because they couldn't even share the paint brushes without poking each other. I got them all on the carpet and put on some meditation

194

music to get them breathing and recalibrated. I think I needed it more than them. I was feeling anxious about this little boy's situation and I didn't need to be here covering a class. I put on some Mozart and the afternoon was going swimmingly until the secretary came into the classroom with two police officers.

The children immediately lost attention on their paintings. I heard one boy saying that they had come to arrest me. I said to him, "Be careful I know what you did at playtime and I'll tell them." He quickly put his head down and got on with his painting. He knew what he had done at playtime.

I went out with the police and left the class with the teaching assistant. As I was talking to them, I could hear the class getting louder and louder and had to keep popping my head in to get them to be quiet. The police officers informed me that the mother would not be released, and they were looking to find relatives to take the boy for the night.

"She was just shoplifting," I said.

"It's not the shoplifting, it's because she's an illegal immigrant," they responded.

This really annoyed me.

I continued, "So because she's an illegal immigrant you are going to separate her from her five-year-old child and keep her in custody for a whole night?"

"We don't make the rules," one of them said.

And he was right, so there was no point for me to continue with this line of enquiry.

"We will be coming back with someone to take him later," the female officer informed me.

I told her our club is open until 6 p.m. and I would wait for them to come back.

The day finished in a blur. I just wanted to get the police off the premises as their presence is always taken as a sign that something bad has happened in the school and I didn't like that. They came back at six but they hadn't found any relatives or friends willing to take the child for the night, so they would have to take him to the station and wait.

We explained to Joshua what would happen, and he seemed happy enough to go with them. He was excited to ride in a police car. However, by the time we got to the police car the novelty had worn off and the reality kicked in for him, so he grabbed hold of my leg and started crying and screaming, "I don't want to go with them, please don't make me go with them." It broke my heart. I explained again why this was happening and tried to reassure him he would be safe, but he was clinging on to my leg for dear life. Of course, he was terrified, and I should have thought of this before I even took him outside. I asked the officers if I could go with him and they agreed. He was happy for me to accompany him.

This was not how I had anticipated my day to go. I called C before I left and said I hoped to be home soon. "Wow in a police car, your day has been worse than mine." As we pulled out of the car park and down the street, I was spotted in the back of the police car by a group of pupils and parents out on the estate. They went crazy when they saw me, yelling and screaming and pointing at me in the car. I could just hear them now, "Mr P was arrested." "What do you think he did?" I laughed as I knew this was going to do wonders for my reputation.

We were taken into a holding room and given some juice. Luckily, I'd grabbed some books, a board game and some colouring pencils to keep us occupied. At first, he was excited as he thought this was a big adventure, but eventually he began to show anxiety and his mother was nowhere to be seen. Every time there was a noise his head turned to the door expecting to see his mother. The duty officer kept popping her head in to check on us and on her last visit she told me that he would have to go into a foster home for the night. I was devastated. No one from his family would come and keep him for the night.

By 9 p.m. he had fallen asleep beside me and I was ready to nod off as well. A few minutes later the duty officer came in with the foster lady and we woke him up to tell him. I explained to Joshua that he would have to go with the lady to her house only for tonight and luckily, she was a sweet and matronly figure who coaxed him by offering him some nice chicken and chips and a video game. He asked me to go with him, but luckily the duty officer stepped in and said that I wanted to, but she wouldn't let me. Thank God for small favours because by this point, I was ready to cry.

I said good night to him, and he gave me a hug. "I'll see you at school tomorrow," I said. He left with the nice matronly lady and I just sat on the chair and put my head in my hands. The police officer was nice to me. She said, "Not many people would do this. You are kind." I sighed and thanked her for her help. As I was about to leave, I realised I didn't even know what police station I was in. I asked her where we were, and she smiled and told me she would call me a cab.

When I got home, C had dinner waiting for me and a tall glass of gin and tonic.

19 January

I didn't sleep all night thinking about how Joshua was doing with the foster family and wondering if his mother will be released from jail. I went into school early and waited with trepidation to see what had happened to him. At 8:30 there was a knock on the door, and I saw Joshua's smiley face with his mother holding his hand. He ran in to my office and gave me a box of chocolates and a little card.

I made a big deal of it and declared, "These are my favourite chocolates. How did you know?"

His smile got even bigger.

I opened the card and saw that he had written a big 'Thank you Mr P' in coloured pencil and signed his name. He told me immediately that he had chicken and chips with Linda (the foster mother) and played a game with her son. I was so relieved he was okay. I told him to go out and play with his friends while I spoke to his mother.

The mother was standing at the door looking very anxious. I offered her a chair to sit down and almost immediately she bursts into tears. I grabbed my handy box of tissues and pushed it towards her. She took one almost automatically even though she had one in her hand already.

199

Before she said anything, I said to her, "Thank you so much for coming in to see me today and bringing Joshua into school. It's the best thing for him."

She was still crying but managed to say, "Thank you for looking after him yesterday. I'm so embarrassed this has happened. I'm sorry. I knew I was going to run out of money, so I put some food in my bag, so I had enough to buy Joshua a treat on the weekend." She didn't even raise her head.

"You don't have to be sorry and I'm not here to judge." I told her I could subsidise Joshua's breakfast club if that would help and she kindly accepted my offer.

I wished her well and I thought she left feeling a bit brighter than when she had come in. Hopefully, she can sort her immigration status out and get on with raising her child. I went to check on Joshua in the playground but he was too busy scoring a goal to even notice me. I was hoping this experience wouldn't be too traumatic for him. It's so hard to tell what will affect children so young. I know somewhere in his subconscious he will have this registered as a sense of abandonment. I wish I could erase it for him. All we can do is make him safe in school and hope that the kindness he encounters in life will be more than the cruelty.

20 January

When I first came to my school there was lots of contention about the sex education lessons, and being a church school there was some taboo around contraception and homosexuality. I was the year 6 teacher and was tasked with the job of delivering them. I went on a course with a wonderful organisation called the Christopher Winter Project and was given amazing support to implement their scheme. It was a time when Section 28 was still in law and everyone was nervous about anything deviating from the norm. The law was named after Section 28 of the Local Government Act of 1988 and stated that a local authority "…shall not intentionally promote homosexuality or publish material with the intention of promoting homosexuality or promote the teaching in any maintained school of the acceptability of homosexuality as a pretended family relationship." This was repealed in 2003 in England. I repeat that for dramatic emphasis, it was repealed in 2003 in England.

My mantra was don't ask for permission if you think you are going to get a no. Being the new teacher gave me ample opportunity to do what I thought was best and if anyone had a problem with that, I would just put my hands up and say, "Well nobody told me that!" So, in my very first year when some in the church were very uneasy about showing children condoms in a sex education lesson or referring to homosexuality as an acceptable model of a loving relationship, I did both. We had a grand old time learning to be safe before we disposed of them into the bin. I counted them to make sure I got back as many as I had given out. The last thing I needed was to find one in the playground. The children didn't bat an eyelid when I discussed homophobic bullying (this was the way to get around any misunderstandings about 'promoting' homosexuality) and when we discussed that some people are attracted to the same sex and we mustn't discriminate against them, it was accepted as the kind and compassionate thing to do. The children are never the problem. It's the parents and the buffoons that make the law that get in the way.

I told the head teacher at the time what I had done, and she almost had a stroke. She told me that the governors had been debating this for years and could not come to a decision. "Sorry," I said, "I'm new and I didn't know that. Just blame it on me!" I think she was secretly relieved that the problem was solved. Nobody broke any laws, and she could just blame it on the new kid on the block. If my legacy will be breaking down the barriers put up by fearful, narrow-minded people, then I'll be happy. Children always give me hope that they are more tolerant of people's differences than adults are.

Today I was having a meeting about our sex and drugs education lessons. First, I never understood why those two were ever joined when referencing sexual relations education. It's as if someone subconsciously was reciting sex, drugs, and rock and roll and stopped at the drugs bit. It's like saying that sex is as bad as taking drugs, or even worse: people who have sex also take drugs.

We briefly discussed the content of the sex education lessons and decided to continue with the anonymous question box at the end of the lessons. Of course, it's never anonymous because we recognise their handwriting, but if they believe they can openly ask questions then job well done. We usually go into my office and read them out. I have to say we have had some crackers over the years and rolled around laughing. I feel bad having to admit to that, but they are funny.

A boy once asked when his 'tentacles' were going to drop. Most of them are just about puberty, hair, masturbation, and wet dreams. At the beginning of every lesson, we try to answer all the questions they have, however, some of them are too explicit to mention. I once had a question about why grown-ups always have sex in pub toilets. I was not going to touch that one, so I rephrased it and discussed that public places are not appropriate places for sex, but sometimes when people are drinking or taking drugs then they are not thinking straight. I guess this is where sex, drugs, and rock and roll need to be discussed.

But my favourite comment came today from a boy in year 6 at the end of our sessions. Once his teacher and I had completed the sessions and discussed contraception etc. we asked them if they have any further questions. He put his hand up quite sheepishly and asked with sheer horror in his eyes, "Do I have to have sex now?" That was priceless! He thought just because the lessons were over (a bit like a driver) he would have to go out and do it. "No," I said to him because it's illegal to do so before the age of sixteen. You would be breaking the law if you did that. Another hand shot up. I didn't anticipate this one.

"But Mr P, my mum had me when she was fifteen, does this mean she broke the law?" he asked.

I thought, *This is turning out to be tricky.*

No sooner did I have this thought than another hand shot up. "Mr P, my daddy was seventeen and my mummy was fifteen when they had me. Can my daddy go to prison?"

I taught her daddy, and he might be going to prison for other reasons but not this one. I did the only thing I could by this point. I refrained from answering any of their questions and just reminded them that our number one rule was that we don't discuss our personal lives or families in these sessions. That quickly put an end to question time. I knew there was good reason I made up that rule.

23 January

Today was quiet in school. I only had one screamer at lunchtime. A little boy in year 1 had fallen over and grazed his knee. He is a real howler. I came out of my office to see what had happened, but quickly saw that it was all superficial and he had already had his magic cold compress of cotton wool. Problem solved.

I went back and continued updating my school development plan. Once you start listing every member of staff that will be involved in these plans, how much each task will cost and timeframes for completion it can turn into an educational *War and Peace*. I must be honest and say that I don't even think I have read all of mine. I merely go in and change it every term to make it look relevant and make sure none of the dates and targets are old. It is merely a pencil and paper exercise to have something to show governors and inspectors. I don't think they have read it in full either. Every head teacher knows what their school needs: quality teaching, exemplary behaviour, good attitudes to learning and risk taking. It's an amazingly simple equation.

If I had spent the time that I have wasted on filling in forms that made no difference to helping children, I would have probably made more of a difference. But I didn't have the courage to do this as there are too many people out there waiting to criticise you for not doing your job properly, and in a setting of high deprivation where the odds are not in your favour, you run the risk of having your career destroyed by a negative report. It's utterly paralysing to feel so much fear, but unfortunately this is the culture we live in and what all schools are facing.

The main problem is that there is a fundamental lack of trust in social institutions. This stems from the top and permeates into every policy made to police every action we take. All of this 'policing' creates an unmanageable amount of fear and in the name of accountability our workload has reached unrealistic levels. When all we can do is talk about people's well-being then we are not managing the expectations very well. These well-being initiatives are nothing but plasters in a system that flagrantly treats people like machines on a production line. It's almost as if you are telling people that it is their fault that they are not managing their well-being when you are demanding the impossible.

24 January

If I can just figure out which game or gadget will be the next best thing in the playground, I can make billions. I like seeing the yo-yo resurface every five years or even the trading cards. We always try to accommodate the children and allow them to bring them into school. Sometimes we need to ban them if they start getting stolen or damaged, but usually it's nice for them to have hobbies and interests that they share with their friends.

I especially liked the craze of the loom bands, which were little plastic bands that children wove into the most intricate bracelets. This one was epic. It became a world-wide phenomenon and then you heard of schools banning them all over the world. Why on Earth would I ban an activity that was creative, helped children concentrate and could be done while they chatted with their friends? My problem was that I couldn't possibly wear all the ones that were given to me as gifts by the children. I would end up looking like a Christmas tree if I wore all of them. I made sure I wore it for the day or the week depending on the colours (hot pink was not my colour).

However, there was one fad that I banned very quickly from my school and luckily it hasn't resurfaced. This was the infamous Tamagotchi. This little device, that was the size of a key chain, was a virtual pet that the children had to take care of. I found it very disconcerting that they were looking after virtual pets and not real ones. They became obsessed with them and even though they were banned in the classroom, they were so small that children were constantly 'feeding' them under their tables and were in a perpetual state of anxiety over their well-being. This was not healthy. They started caring more for these Tamagotchis than they did for their own siblings. During one of my observation weeks, I confiscated about a dozen of them. The rule was that they could not have them back until their parents collected them.

Unfortunately, I forgot to take them out of my jacket pocket and ended up going home with them. Unbeknownst to me these little pets would start to die if they were not fed or watered and they would let out an electronic wail while they were dying. At about 3 a.m. on a Saturday morning I was woken up by the most hideous sound and didn't know where it was coming from. I tracked it to my hallway closet and discovered it was coming from my jacket. I couldn't shut them up and no matter where I stored them, I could hear them. I made the decision to free them into the wild, so I put them in a bag and threw them outside in the bins.

On the Monday morning I had a few parents come in with their children to claim them back and I told them that I am sorry, but their pet died peacefully over the weekend and I gave them a proper burial.

RIP.

26 January

This morning a boy in year 6 told a new girl from Nigeria to go back to her country. His teacher sent him to me for a chat because he was also mocking her accent. I looked at Abraham as he came through my door and could only wonder what made him say such mean things to Christine. I personally think he likes her and doesn't know how else to get her attention, but I have a zero tolerance for any forms of racial discrimination.

"Did you tell her to go back to her country, Abraham?"

He nodded and wouldn't even look at me.

"Did you make fun of the way she speaks English?"

He nodded again. At least he wasn't denying it.

I asked him the obvious, "Where is your family from, Abraham?"

He answered in the smallest of voices, "Nigeria."

"Can you then explain to me why you think it's okay to tell Christine to go back to Nigeria, when that's exactly where your family came from?" I asked him and now I could feel my blood boiling.

His answer was not a surprise to me. "Because my parents said that they just come here for benefits and take money from us."

It was phenomenal how utterly absurd it was for migrant groups to try and exclude other migrant groups from opportunities they once benefitted in receiving.

I didn't think I was ever going to get Abraham to understand these subtle race relations, but I was damn sure he was going to understand that comments like these are racist.

He quickly said, "But I'm Nigerian too, so it doesn't count."

For that comment I invited his parents in after school and I made him repeat every word he said to me including what his parents had said at home. You could hear a pin drop in the room. I made it even more uncomfortable when I told them that Abraham will now be put on the racist incident register and monitored. (I make it sound more formal than it is, but it seems to prick up the whole family's ears.) I warned him in front of his parents that if he repeats such language then he will have a 2-day exclusion, and this will go on his record.

None of them were happy, but I really didn't care, they needed to learn to keep their bigotry to themselves. I knew I wasn't going to change the parents' beliefs, but maybe I could start to chip away at Abraham's views of the world.

This reminded me of how I grew up in Chicago in the 1970s and 1980s. These decades had their own sets of changes and social upheavals. School was a tricky time. Like many immigrant families my parents had a restaurant, but unlike other families we didn't live in an immigrant neighbourhood and we rarely socialised with others from our country apart from our relatives. This did not mean we assimilated. We were immigrants after all. The Americans were referred to by my family as the foreigners. That was sweet coming from the economic migrants themselves, but everyone was really from somewhere else, so we retained the right to feel superior to everyone else.

At school I was the foreigner. I was often told to go back to my country and never invited to other children's birthday parties. Other children laughed at me when my mother would pick me up after school and speak in a foreign language. We lived in the city of Chicago, but in an exclusively white neighbourhood. My brother and I were part of a handful of foreigners in the school, and we were constantly reminded of this in so many traumatising but also defining ways. As I've said my brother was very naughty. I was always apologising for him and trying to overcompensate by being the hardworking student.

At the start of every new school year, I was faced with the same scene. Once the teacher reached my name on the attendance register, she would stop and even gasp at times. She would turn into a lighter shade of Casper and look up at me and utter those infamous words, "Are you George's brother?" I felt sorry for them as I knew the sheer horror must have shaved some years off their lives. I had the same answer. "Yes miss, but you will soon realise that I am nothing like my delinquent brother." I was always hoping that my use of the word 'delinquent' would impress them. I think it probably took weeks before they believed me and began to breathe easy again and stopped watching their backs.

The only teacher that didn't react in this way was Miss Metzinger. She was hard as nails and would never show any fear. She just looked at me over her glasses and probably thought, "I know how to bring your family down." I once had a mini revolution and she

211

squashed it immediately. At the time my parents were trying to become American citizens and there was lots of stress in the house. My mother's English was terrible, and she had to pass a citizenship test before we could become citizens. It was a gruelling six months trying to teach my mother, whose English ranged from good morning, good evening and have a nice day, the ins and outs of the US constitution and structures of government.

I must have been feeling some residual resentment at being an immigrant and staged my first political protest. Every morning all children in the U.S. stand up, face the flag, put their right hand on their heart and recite in unison the Pledge of Allegiance, followed by the singing of the national anthem. I decided I would not stand for either of these on this day. I managed to get away with it unnoticed until we were singing the national anthem. Every morning Miss Metzinger would play the piano and we would all sing along to her shrill voice. Halfway through she must have noticed that I wasn't standing and suddenly, she slammed her hands on the piano making the loudest of noises. Some children jumped in fright.

She stood up to her full stature (she was a tall woman with fiery red hair and a very scary voice) and addressed me directly with my last name, "P…why are you not standing?" Every eye in the room was on me now. Some faces looked on in sheer horror at this act of insanity.

I gave her my pre-prepared reply, "Because I'm not American, Miss Metzinger, and until I get my citizenship, I won't be pledging allegiance or singing."

There you go!

Now this was 1982 and political correctness had yet to hit our shores.

She responded emphatically, "Get up now or I'll put you back on that boat where you came from!"

Suffice to say that my revolution was squashed, and I stood up and sang like a canary. She moved my seat the next day making sure I was sitting next to her on the piano. My political protest had landed me in hot water. I had to endure this woman's spit on my face for the rest of the year. I think she purposely projected it in my direction. However, I had earned the respect of the people. My peers couldn't believe I had staged my protest, and it was all they could talk about for weeks in the playground. I was a hero in their eyes and my actions would be what urban myths are made of. I dared to defy Miss Metzinger (the dragon lady) and lived to tell the tale. I didn't even mind that I had to sit next to her for the rest of the year. I wore it as a badge of honour.

For years in Elementary school my teachers thought I was a genius. This was because every year my test scores on basic skills in English were about ten years ahead of my age group. They couldn't understand how this immigrant boy, whom they thought spoke English as a second language (I'm bilingual) could have these inexplicably high results. They just put it down to innate genius and didn't even bother teaching me most of the time. I was always given independence as they assumed I could do it all. What they failed to recognise was that speaking another language immediately increased my active vocabulary in English. I could identify words beyond my age group solely because I knew them in my native language. I never bothered to tell them this because it gave me the stature I needed as an immigrant.

This status of the political hero with the beautiful mind would come to a crashing halt one day during lunch. My parents would never allow us to eat any cafeteria food or even go to anyone else's home for lunch or dinner. We either had packed lunch full of home cooking or came home for grandmother to cook us a fresh meal. Going to McDonalds was like smuggling in contraband. You'd think we were taking drugs if my dad ever got a whiff of us eating anything but his restaurant food or my mother's cooking. One day I brought home a classmate for lunch. It was winter and my grandmother had prepared a traditional goat soup. The only problem was that the soup contained the goat's head. It hadn't occurred to me that I would need to warn my friend of this culinary experience.

My grandmother put the pot on the table and once she took off the lid, my brother and I dove into the head in earnest. So here we are with two boys ripping out a goat's tongue and playing tug of war with it and an American boy brought up on hot dogs and hamburgers getting paler and paler. Suddenly, we heard a 'thump', and this stopped the battle. My grandmother was screaming as she tried to bring him round and my brother just threw his drink on his face. Thankfully, he wasn't out for long. My grandmother was trying to explain to him that it's just a goat and this is what we eat in our country and that she could make him a peanut butter and jelly sandwich if he wanted. I think she was just scaring him even more with her thick accent and crazy eyes. She told me to take him back to school and make sure I bought him a hot dog on the way. I had lost the tongue. My brother picked it up off the floor and was already eating it. She gave us some money and we walked back to school in silence.

Within 24 hours I went from hero to freak. His harrowing accounts of lunch inclusive of tongues, brains and eyeballs had branded us as the cannibals. We never got invited to sleepovers, birthday parties or after school playdates. I went from Che Guevara to Hannibal Lecter. I was once again the dirty foreigner and just played with the only other foreigner in my class, a boy from India. However, this was all about to change with desegregation of schools…

As a predominantly white school, my school was chosen to participate in Chicago's desegregation programme. As I look back on it now, I'm astounded that we were using words like desegregation in the 1980s, but, unfortunately, while laws may have changed in the 1950s and 1960s, the real change took decades to happen, if it has happened at all.

One September day we had yellow school buses parked in rows in front of the school bringing children from overcrowded inner-city schools. This was epic for me. I will not lie I was no longer the only ethnic minority in my class. The spotlight was finally off me. I was excited. I saw these fellow students as kindred spirits and went out of my way to welcome them and show them the ropes of our school.

The only problem with this system was that I never got to see my new friends after school. They would immediately be on their buses at the end of the day and off they went to their homes in the city. The descriptions of their living conditions always left me feeling scared for them. They would tell me that on some nights the police sirens would never stop. They all had seen a gun and heard it being shot and some had even seen and taken drugs. For a twelve-year-old this was too much life, too soon. I was lucky. I lived in a relatively safe neighbourhood, my parents had a business and they shielded us from a lot of the horrors of the outside world.

I never found out what happened to my friends. I looked for them online but haven't found a trace of them. On the other hand, I can find all my white friends bar one. It's like they only existed in that inner city that I never visited because it was a bus ride too far.

I can't help but reflect on the school I lead today and look at my pupils to see how this subtle segregation still exists. There are state schools with predominantly white, middle-class children and others with black and white British disadvantaged children. What is most shocking and possibly even worse is that these children live in the same neighbourhoods. Why doesn't anybody in education want to address this issue? Ask any head teacher and they would confirm this. It is an inconvenient truth for policy makers and leaders to expose this blatant manipulation of the freedom to choose your school. It would lose them votes to try and address this inequality. Sometimes the freedom to choose only benefits those that see the choices and can make them.

1 February

Today was a late one. We had parents' evening until 7 p.m. I walked around the school greeting parents that were waiting to see the teachers and just had some chats with them about their children. We didn't get most of the parents in and that made me sad. Every year I try to drum up interest, but I can't seem to crack that one.

At 6 p.m. I made my way to my office as a parent had made an appointment to see me, and all she said to the school admin officer when she made the appointment was that it's confidential. This worried me as I can never anticipate what confidential means. She was already waiting for me when I got there. I asked her to come in and sit down. To my relief she just wanted me to help her fill in an application online for her daughter, which needed my reference. So, we sat in front of my computer and started filling it in. At some point I noticed out of the corner of my eye that something was moving under her sweater. I tried to ignore it, but it was very disconcerting. She was constantly shifting on her chair and adjusting her sweater. At some point I could hear a strange sound coming out of her sweater and she was trying desperately to conceal it by coughing. When I turned to her to ask her some details for the application, I noticed that the movement had exponentially increased and the scene now looked like the one in *Alien* when the creature came out of Sigourney Weaver's stomach. Again, I pretended not to notice as

I didn't want to make a reference to what's under someone's sweater and I continued with the application. But I was so distracted that I had to say something.

"I'm really sorry, but I think we need to address the elephant in the room," I said trying to make light of it.

"I really don't know what you mean," she said rather curtly.

What could I do now? I couldn't go ahead and ask her to reveal what she was concealing under her sweater because that would be very awkward to say the least. I turned back to the application and tried to finish it as quickly as I could. As I was about to press submit on the application, I asked her to look have a look at all the details and make sure we hadn't missed anything. As we both stood up to swap places, so she could see the computer, the chihuahua she was hiding under her sweater dropped to the floor and started barking like mad.

We both just stared at it and then I said, "So, this is the elephant in the room." She could have suffocated the poor thing.

She said, "I do this all the time, but usually he's in my handbag."

I can't deal with this level of crazy at the end of a long day, so I just pressed submit and sent her on her way.

3 February

Every Friday we finish off our week with a celebration assembly. The whole school comes together, and we celebrate all the wonderful work the children have completed. We sing happy birthday and then we revisit our Christian theme for the half-term. But Fridays can sometimes trigger some inexplicable behaviour from children and parents. I don't know if it's the anticipation of spending two whole days together that drives them crazy or just the end of an incredibly stressful week.

Today we came out of the hall to find three police vans outside the gate and about a dozen police officers trying to stop a riot. I ran out to see what had happened and I was faced with a barrage of screaming parents asking me to resolve the conflict. I didn't even know what was going on, let alone how to solve it. It is phenomenal that the parents immediately turn to me to solve it and take full responsibility as if I have the power to wave a magic wand and stop it all from happening. Last time I checked I was not a law enforcement officer or a genie.

It turned out that Charlie's mum came to confront Hakan's mum about Hakan jostling Charlie's grandmother on the bus. How ridiculous! Hakan's mum doesn't speak any English, and this seemed to enrage Charlie's mum, who had done this before on the school premises. She is a hothead. Today she crossed the line.

219

Charlie's mum lunged at Hakan's mum and was out of control. Other parents called the police and then it escalated because she was making nasty racist comments while she was lunging at her. The other parents didn't take kindly to being called racist names, so they surrounded her and her family.

This was when we come out with our certificates, stickers, and balloons after talking about our Christian value of peace. There is nothing worse than busting your backside to improve standards and create a safe and welcoming environment for your children to then have a riot just outside your gates. Sometimes I feel like I'm fighting a losing battle. It's embarrassing to be the school in the community with the most police visits in the year.

I tried desperately to disperse the crowd and quickly moved all the involved parties into the school hall. This seemed to do the trick and most families moved on. I also asked the police officer to turn off the flashing lights as this seemed to attract the most attention. He kindly obliged and we went into the hall to sort the mess out.

Charlie's mum had already left and there was a police car going around her house. I assumed they would arrest her, but I didn't have a chance to ask the police. My main concern was Hakan's mum, who was looking pretty shaken up. I got her a cup of tea and left her to give her statement to the police officers. One of them asked me for all the families' details and I went to the office with her to write it all down. I explained to her that it wasn't the first time something like this had happened and she asked me to put it all in a statement. That took another hour and by this point I had lost the will to live.

I was simply happy it was the weekend.

6 February

Charlie didn't come to school today and I think it was the best thing for him after how his mother behaved on Friday. It would be so difficult for that little boy to come back and face all his friends. At midday I got a call from another head teacher in a neighbouring school informing me that Charlie and his mum rocked up first thing this morning asking for a place and claiming that they wanted to move schools because I had banned her and Charlie from coming onto the premises. What a bloody cheek! That was very stupid of her. Didn't she think that head teachers speak to each other? I explained to my colleague how ridiculous her claims were and reassured her that the child is an absolute delight and maybe it would be best for him to have a fresh start where nobody knows what a maniac his mother is.

It's not long now before my year 6 teacher goes on maternity leave and I have yet to find a replacement. I have advertised twice and gone through three agencies. I'm starting to have restless nights worrying about getting the children a good teacher before they take their SATs tests. This is such a crucial time for our children and the slightest change can have a profound impact on their emotional well-being.

I think I'm going to have to put my deputy head teacher in there at least until the SATs tests. This way I can ensure the children will have someone with them that they know and trust. We are continuously humiliated in these annually published league tables, which say nothing of a school's character or obstacles we face to attain these results. They do not attest to the lack of life experiences our 'inner city' pupils have, to meet the expectations of a predominantly middle-class test.

My children have all the intelligence of any of the middle-class 'shire' children but lack the approved vocabulary that is expected of them. When they are faced with a reading booklet full of experiences of white, middle-class children, they struggle to find any common experiences with these stories. They do not have stories of idyllic countryside scenes where two seemingly affluent white children are rowing on a lake in pursuit of their next summer break adventure.

This is only one example of the type of text they are asked to comprehend: "Ripples of water fanned out behind them as they crossed the glassy surface of the lake."

In another text where a white girl in an African game park (how colonial!) steps out in secret to ride one of the giraffes, she encounters some warthogs. The baby warthogs are described in the following way, "There she dangled while Jemmy pranced skittishly and the warthog, intent on defending her young, let out enraged squeals from below. Five baby warthogs milled around in bewilderment, spindly tails pointing heavenwards." The question the children were asked was: "...milled around in bewilderment" (page 8). Explain what this description suggests about the baby warthogs."

Are you kidding me? You are asking the poorest, most inexperienced children in the country to understand and articulate what 'milled around in bewilderment' means and then proceed to judge them from the age of 11 based on their answer and similar answers to copious amounts of ill-conceived questions on ridiculous tests? This is preposterous.

We are setting children up to fail when they can succeed and should succeed. We set obstacles through testing systems that only prove that affluence and life experience will get you further in life than your peers. We know that already. We also proceed to judge, name and shame schools and hardworking professionals to the point where they are leaving the profession in droves.

How do you solve the problem?

<u>A very modest proposal to improve the quality of education in the United Kingdom:</u>

Start the formal national curriculum at the age of 7. That's the age children are ready to learn in a formal setting.

Invest in high-quality Early Years provision from the age of 2-7. Let children play and learn from each other and stop testing them.

Make Nurseries free for all from the age of 2.

Fund parents properly to stay at home for the first year of a child's life. Legislate so that women are not penalised from work for having a family.

Start teachers' salaries at £40,000 and get this money by abolishing organisations like Ofsted and divert money from the Defence budget. We have enough weapons to blow each other up too many times. Adding to it doesn't make us safer.

Test only to find out how to help children not how to penalise schools.

Create a national education publishing house full of the greatest minds and best practitioners and roll out high-quality books, plans and schemes for schools to use free of charge. This should be politics free and not changeable after every election.

Insist that families take their children to the local school. Free choice has led to pockets of segregation. Only if your local school is full should you look at the next closest. Spread the diversity.

Get rid of local authority consultants who do nothing but push paper and create more work for head teachers and employ school-based social workers and counsellors.

Proper funds for children with special needs and disabilities to have access to specialist teachers who can include them appropriately. Increase the number of special schools attached to mainstream schools, so that the children with the highest needs can have access to high-quality provision.

8 February

David came to me this morning already in a bad mood and in trouble for throwing a pencil at one of his classmates. We had a long chat about how he was feeling, but how do you explain to a child who is on the autistic spectrum, has ADHD, has suffered from trauma and has gone to four different schools by the age of eleven that he needs to cooperate with the teacher and his peers?

His world is an enclosed bubble of self-preservation that does not follow the expected rules of engagement. I learned very quickly with David that my normal head teacher's 'strict' voice is not going to work with him. He just gets angrier and angrier and winds himself up to such a frenzy that he gets out of control. He's a tricky case because he's very articulate and has got into a pattern of blaming everyone else for his problems.

I asked him if he had breakfast and that's all it took for him to go off on a tirade. It's like he gets on an imaginary soap box and begins a barrage of complaints. Sometimes he even jumps up to have a go at me.

"Why do you people always ask me about my breakfast?" he shouted at me.

He always calls us 'you people'. This is direct parroting from how he hears his mum referring to us. Many children do this, and it saddens me to think that we are constantly seen as the enemy.

His voice got higher. "You're not my family. Leave me alone."

Frank, his 1:1 assistant, calmly responded to him, "It's because we care about you and want you to have a good start to the day."

His response was cutting. "Are you my father? No, you're not my father. Go feed your own children. Oh, I forgot you don't have any. What gives you the right to tell me what to do, man?"

I asked him what he thinks we should do now.

His answer almost made me laugh. "I don't know you're the one being paid to be the head teacher. Why are you asking me to do your job?"

"Okay then I'll give you two choices. A: You go back to class, apologise to your teacher for disrupting the class and check on your classmate to see if he's okay. Or B: I call your mother and we wait for her to show up and see if she agrees with you that it's okay to throw a pencil at someone just because you didn't like it," I said.

He thought about it for a minute and he tried to negotiate with me. My thought is, *If this kid can finish school and keep his cool, he can negotiate a better Brexit deal than our government.*

He started, "What if I apologise to my teacher but not to Kyle? He did it on purpose and always gives me the smallest pencil. That's not fair."

I came back with my counter-offer: "If I make sure that Frank always has a pencil to give you that isn't small, will you agree to apologise? I am being fair by not punishing you right now. All I want is for you to accept responsibility. And before you go on about Kyle's responsibility for giving you a small pencil; that does not excuse you throwing it in his face. This is my final offer. Take it or leave it."

There was a small pause. I could almost hear the showdown music in my head.

"Fine," he said rather reluctantly. "Can I go back to my class now?"

I smiled at him. "Of course, you can. Would you like a piece of fruit before you go?"

I had a bowl of fruit on the table from a breakfast meeting. He took a banana and went to leave. Frank stopped him and reminded him of his manners. He turned around sharply, "Thank you, Mr P," he said. I think I saw his shoulders relax. At least I got him to eat something. He might make it to lunch now.

9 February

Ifeoma in year 5 disclosed to us yesterday that her father and grand-mother, who were abroad, died yesterday. I tried calling her mother to speak to her, but I couldn't get an answer, so I just left her a message for her to come and see me first thing today. My heart was racing as I didn't know what state I'd find her in. What do you say to someone who's just lost two members of her family? My approach was to focus on the child's needs and how we could support her in school. One of her classmates, who lost her dad last year, was brave and looked after her yesterday. I know it wasn't easy for her as it brought back many unhappy memories, but she was so compassionate, and I was very proud of her.

I saw mum waiting at the door, so I didn't hesitate to go and greet her. She had a worried look on her face and I couldn't blame her. I asked her to sit down and I made sure that the box of tissues were in the centre of the table as always.

I began by saying, "First, I would like to say thank you for coming in as I understand this must be a difficult time for you and your family."

She didn't respond, but I wasn't expecting her to say anything.

So, I continued in earnest, "I just want to reassure you that we are here for Ifeoma and all your family and we will support her as best as we can in school. We can also seek any support from outside agencies if needed. I think it would be best to just see how she is over the next few weeks, and we can keep in touch and share any observations on how she is feeling. If we notice anything concerning, then we can have another meeting and maybe discuss a plan forward. I think in these circumstances it's best to be guided by the child."

"Mr P, what are you talking about?" she said rather bluntly.

I was shocked she should ask me this, so I replied, "I'm referring to the loss of her your husband and his mother recently."

"My husband and his mother are in Lagos and they are not lost," she said with a quizzical look on her face.

"But Ifeoma told us that they died a couple of days ago."

I could see the horror in her eyes. "They are not dead, Mr P. They are in Lagos alive and well, God bless them."

She took out her phone and called her husband.

"That's not necessary, ma'am, I believe you…" But it was no use the phone was ringing.

She talked to her husband in Yoruba and I could only understand the interspersed English words like 'dead' and 'God' and 'school'. After what seemed like a very heated conversation, she put the phone down and declared, "I want to see Ifeoma now. Bring her here and we will talk to her."

I had no choice, so I asked the admin officer to call her down.

"I'm so sorry this happened," I said.

"Don't be sorry, they are still alive," she said and I almost burst out laughing.

"I am going to kill her," she announced, but I didn't need to say to her that it's not necessary, I knew she wouldn't.

There was a knock on my door and Ifeoma came in. She looked sad and her eyes were red from crying. She stood in the doorway but didn't see her mother, who was obscured by the door. Part of me wanted to warn her to drop the act, but I couldn't with her mother watching me.

I just blurted out, "Come in Ifeoma, I'm here with your mother," and I pointed to the far corner of the room.

She popped her head around the door and saw her mother. The look she gave Ifeoma was terrifying. I did not envy her. She made the right choice and sat on the far end of the table away from her mother. I could just imagine her mother jumping over the table to get to her and me jumping in to stop her.

I quickly took control of the situation because I could see the mother was getting angrier and angrier. She was even making grunting noises to show Ifeoma how angry she was.

I began, "Ifeoma, why did you tell us that your father and grand-mother died?"

I didn't need to say any more. Her mother launched in with a barrage of abuse. Fifteen minutes later she ran out of steam, took a breath and then announced, "Let's call your father and speak to him from the grave." She took out her phone and pressed his number. All I could understand again was 'Ifeoma', 'dead' and 'God'. She slid the phone across the table and Ifeoma picked it up. I couldn't make out what her dad was saying, but I could hear he was yelling.

Her mother was screaming across the table, "Tell him. Tell him how he died."

Fifteen minutes later and a bucket of tears from Ifeoma and I think her parents were finished, for now. I didn't envy her when she got home tonight. I took over again because I needed to diffuse this now.

"Why did you tell us that your dad and grandma died?" I asked.

"Because I wanted attention," she didn't say that, but I knew that's what she was thinking. She didn't say anything and kept staring at the floor. Her tears were rolling down her cheeks and dripping onto her lap. She didn't even bother to wipe them. I leaned over the table and grabbed the box of tissues I had so carefully placed for her mother and handed her one. I wasn't prepared for this turn of events. She took it reluctantly, as her mother continued making those grunting noises indicating that she was still very angry.

I dispensed with the questioning and just gave her my version of events.

"Did you think that by telling us this you would get as much attention as Hayley did last year when her father died?" I asked her. She nodded and her mother confirmed her dissatisfaction with another guttural grunt. This was too much to handle right now, so I made a suggestion to both of them.

"I think Ifeoma recognises the mistake she made and how many people she upset, especially Hayley who showed her such kindness and compassion. I suggest we leave it here for now and later in the day we will speak to Hayley together and you can apologise. I'm sure you will continue to discuss this at home." At this point, I looked at Mum and she was still not happy, but I think she was less angry. I did not want to be in Ifeoma's shoes when she got home. She was going to get an earful (and rightly deserved).

Mum thanked me and before she left, she took one look at Ifeoma and said, "I'll be back." That sounded like the terminator.

I walked with Ifeoma back to her class just to let her know I was on her side and before she went in, I told her not to worry, I would sort it out with Hayley. I spared her the embarrassment of confessing to Hayley and spoke to her myself. Thankfully, Hayley was very understanding and when they met later in the playground Ifeoma apologised and gave Hayley a hug.

I realised it was almost lunchtime now and that was the only thing I had dealt with all morning. I was not opening my e-mails. I didn't want to have a stroke.

10 February

Today I decided to accompany the children to an indoor tennis tournament. We are proud of our tennis achievements and have won many local and city-wide tournaments. We've even had children compete internationally. This is mainly down to the extra funding I use from the sports grant, and luckily one of my teaching assistants is a tennis coach, so I give her some dedicated time to coach the more talented tennis players. Every year we find ourselves competing with the more affluent schools in the borough, who get mummy and daddy to give them private tuition. Those children come with such confidence and some even have an entourage of coaches. My children come with heart and grit, and today they had me as their cheerleader. I can be very loud.

The boys' events were first, and I knew that our boys were the weakest link of the team. They spectacularly lost the first two matches, but they did come up with some innovative shots. One of them even swapped hands to get to a ball and hit it spectacularly through his legs. At least they didn't give up. They ran down every ball and what they lacked in experience they made up for in tenacity. They miraculously won their last match down to a series of lucky wild shots that just landed on the line and their sheer physical prowess to never give up. I was so proud of them and I was hoarse by the end of their three rounds.

The girls were in a league of their own and we had a chance of winning the trophy this year. After lunch they found themselves in both the individual and team finals. This was turning out to be a cracker of a day. On top of everything, for the first time nobody called me from school with any disasters to solve. "These days are what dreams are made of," I blissfully mused while I sat in my corner waving my imaginary pom poms.

As expected, we were down to the last two teams. I know I tell the children that it doesn't matter what place they get, but secretly I wanted them to win. I looked around the court and we were the only school with black children in a sea of white faces. This says it all. Of course, I wanted them to win. Of course, I wanted them to know that their efforts and talents were worthwhile. Of course, I wanted them to learn the lesson that they can compete and beat the best of the best. They needed this. The school needed this. I needed this. So here we go…

It was down to the two best players from each school and the competition was fierce. The other player had an entourage to even carry her towel. Our girl had me in her corner. I had thrown away all pretence by this point and screamed like a banshee after every winning shot. I even think I caught myself celebrating when the other girl was out. I had to check myself at this point as people were watching me and they all knew I was the head teacher. The score was tied, and our girl was serving. If she won this point, we would win the tournament and the all-around individual title. The point was epic. I think there were about fifteen shots shared between them. I lost count after a while. A weak return from the other player sent a ball short and our girl pounced on it and slammed it back into her opponent's body. She had no chance to even move out of the way.

We were victorious! I gave her the thumbs up and screamed, "You did it!" She approached the net to congratulate her opponent. Unfortunately, her opponent had just thrown a massive strop and was crying hysterically while her entourage consoled her. The referee was brilliant. She reminded the other girl that she needed to congratulate the winner, but she refused. I was livid. I was having an out of body experience and I could see myself marching over to that smug entourage and giving them a piece of my mind. But then our girl did something I will never forget. She put her hand out over the net and just kept it there waiting for the girl to come and shake it. I was so proud of her it almost brought me to tears.

"Don't you dare move your hand," I commanded telepathically. "You keep it there until that smug prima donna comes and shakes it."

And she did exactly that. When the entourage saw that our girl was not going to have her moment stolen by a tantrum, they coaxed her into reluctantly coming up and shaking her hand.

This moment for me was a double triumph. We had managed to win the girls' trophy, but more importantly we had given our children the opportunity to dream big. To say to themselves as Barack Obama said to a generation of people, "Yes we can!" And we did. We won't always win big and indeed the losses are many. However, we build and build and get stronger and stronger until one day we prove to our children and ourselves that hard work, perseverance, and hope can all come together to achieve success. I'm sure she will take this experience and carry it with her for the rest of her life. It might even define who she becomes and how far she goes. It fills my heart with such joy to think that we have played a small part in that journey.

14 February

The children have started celebrating Valentine's Day. I hate it!

When I was growing up in the USA we had to bring in Valentine's cards to all our classmates. How ridiculous. In theory it's nice to think that everyone was included, but do you really think that children were not going to find a way to differentiate the real ones from the fake ones? Of course, they did. They bedazzled the ones that were really meant for their Valentine. I remember how crushed my best friend Kevin was when the girl he'd loved for all his ten years just signed her name to the card with no hint of any romance in the horizon. Her affections were only directed to Greg the jock, along with every other girl in the class. Let's hope that Greg lost his hair quickly and gained forty pounds right after high school. Try explaining this tradition to your immigrant parents who looked at you blankly when you said, "I need thirty Valentine cards," and my mom responds, "What? For the boys too?"

So here I am almost forty years later, and this greeting card holiday has crossed the Atlantic through the power of soppy American television series that have infiltrated the mass European consciousness. I am now having to take a stand on Valentine's cards and I unequivocally banned them. I didn't discuss it. I didn't consult on it with anyone. I just made an executive decision as the head teacher (we do have that right sometimes) to veto this ridiculous occasion.

That evening as I found myself picking up chocolates and flowers for C, I told myself that I was not a hypocrite and that I had done the children a favour for not exposing them to rejection so soon in their lives. My executive decision stands. Sometimes you just need to follow your gut. I draw the line at buying a card tonight. I'm no sell-out.

16 February

We had a first aid course for all the staff today. I understand that we need to be trained on the serious stuff, like keeping a child alive if they're not breathing, but all my staff care about is whether it's okay to use cotton wool on an open wound. They fail to understand the enormity of a life-or-death situation. This is my worst fear as a head teacher. I thank God every day when the children have gone home safely and return in good health the next day. As the instructor advised us to never attend any open wounds without gloves, I recall the most horrific medical emergency when I was a teacher years ago.

It was the end of lunchtime play and I was going up the stairs to my classroom. It was raining that day so the children had 'wet play', and this meant they would be climbing the walls all afternoon, so I braced myself for what state I would find my classroom in. As I approached the top of the landing, I heard the door slam loudly and then what followed I can only describe as a primal howl. Samuel got his finger jammed in the door and he fell into me screaming in agony. He was holding his hand and when I looked down, I noticed the top of his index finger was hanging off a thread of skin.

I grabbed his hand immediately to apply pressure and stop the bleeding. I could tell he was starting to go into shock, so I sat him down in case he passed out and got a teaching assistant to call for an ambulance.

A few minutes later the head teacher came over and her first comment was, "You shouldn't have touched his hand without putting gloves on."

You must be kidding me! I thought, but the look I must have given her probably conveyed my sentiments better. She backed off immediately.

Luckily, Samuel didn't pass out and the bleeding was under control by the time the paramedics arrived. I explained to them what had happened, and they told me that I couldn't let go until we reached the hospital, and a surgeon could see it. We couldn't get hold of his mother, but the head told me she would continue calling her and let me know.

While we were in the ambulance his adrenalin started wearing off and he started to cry and wriggle in extreme pain. I was starting to worry that he might pull on his finger and I was afraid of applying any more pressure. The paramedics gave him some laughing gas to distract him and within a few minutes Samuel was hysterically laughing. I asked for some laughing gas too as my adrenalin had started to wear off, but they refused. At least he was okay now. When we got to the hospital we were fast tracked through A&E and a doctor was waiting for us. At this point I was told I could let go. As I let go of his hand, I felt all the energy drain out of me completely and a nurse led me to a toilet to clean myself up. I tried to get most of the blood off, but I noticed it had dripped all over my clothes and shoes.

Damn it, another perfectly good pair of shoes destroyed. I am going to start wearing trainers to work, I thought.

After some time, the doctor came out to tell me that they would need to operate to reattach the finger. I told him that I was only his teacher so we would have to wait until his mother arrived to give consent. I called the school to enquire what was happening and the head teacher told me that they got hold of her at work, but she would not be able to get here until she finished her shift at 5 p.m. By now it was 3 p.m.

I kept Samuel company on the ward and tried to distract him with various games that I could think of. Luckily, I always have books in my bag, so I read him a few chapters from our class novel. His mother arrived at 6:30 p.m. She said that the bus was late. I was exhausted and just wanted to go home. I wished Samuel well and told him that he was a very brave boy. The doctor came in and took over.

I got home at abouts seven thirty. I called C on the way home to explain what had happened. I forgot about all the blood, and when I got into the house, I caught a glimpse of myself in the mirror. It looked like I had just returned home from a tour of duty. I went straight into the bathroom and stripped out of my blood-stained clothes and took a long hot shower. I hadn't noticed that C had taken the clothes and put them in the washing machine. I was going to throw them away. I slumped into the sofa and turned into liquid. I became one with the cushion. Thank God I had explained most of it over the phone because I was in no fit state to go through it all over again.

Luckily, the neurosurgeon was able to reattach Samuel's finger as the blood flow had not been cut off. Thank God I hadn't let go of his finger. A few months later we had a solicitor's notice that Mum was suing us for negligence. This is the 'No win, No fee' generation. We usually get at least one a year. There was no thank you for holding on to his finger until we reached the hospital. No thank you for sitting with him until she came to the hospital. No thank you for caring for him when he started crying. What a slap in the face.

20 February

It's half-term this week and I went into school today to do some uninterrupted paperwork. I still haven't found a decent year 6 teacher to cover for the maternity leave, so this means my deputy head will have to go into class full-time. This sucks for me, but the children must come first. I will have to pick up everything now at least until the SATs. Once that's out of the way we can find a sports teacher that can just come in and do outdoor activities with them. It's rotten to think that we are so consumed with these SATs tests that we wait until May to relax. Personally, I don't relax until the first week of July when the results are published.

The grounds are looking beautiful. It's a sunny day and I sat outside in the garden to have some lunch. The perennials are starting to shoot up. Some daffodils and snow drops have come up and it's all starting to feel a bit like spring is on its way. I'm glad that it's not dark by four anymore. Yesterday I noticed that the park closing time had been changed to 5:15 p.m. This lifted my spirits.

We have finished half the school year. It feels marvellous to know that we are halfway there. But I can't help but worry about what that means. Halfway until the summer holidays? Halfway until the only decision I need to make on some days is whether I go for a swim or take a nap? Halfway to having a good night's sleep without the night sweats caused by the endless worry about someone's welfare? Halfway to having that healthy glow of a sun-tan? But 'halfway' is also halfway to another year gone. Halfway to wishing our lives away. I'm pleased went come in today, because I need to come when it's this quiet to realise that I would hate it if I didn't have the hustle and bustle of the children to make the day fly by. We are lucky to be here, and we are even luckier to have them in our lives.

27 February

I took my school councillors on a visit to the Houses of Parliament today. They arrange tours for schools, but the quality is usually hit or miss depending on the tour leader. Our guy today was a lanky, awkward-looking man who stuttered quite a bit. Let's call him Mr Bean. He did not have a clue that my children were bored to death within the first twenty minutes. The tour was ninety minutes long. We were not going to make it. My children were so polite and respectful. I love the way they are so loud and boisterous in school and when we take them on a trip, they always have a sense of awe and wonder at the new things they see. They were quietly listening to him, but I didn't think they were getting much out of it. I asked him if we could just pick up the pace and go to the Commons and Lords Chambers.

It was like I asked him to split the atom.

He stuttered all the way through his response, "Well…you see…we have a strict protocol…to follow…and there is a queue to go through…and set times…we can enter each room…"

"Okay don't worry," I said.

I think he was ready to have a stroke. I could see little droplets of sweat forming on his brow and his ears turned bright red. At least we got his blood pumping today. To be fair to him, my intervention did wake him up and he was a bit more animated. Eventually we reached the chambers, but no one could sit down. I understand the MPs and Lords would not want thousands of people sitting in their seats all day long. They would get destroyed. The children were asked if they had any questions.

At this point, Malik put his hand up and asked the most pertinent question: "If MPs are elected to represent us and work together for democracy, that's what our head teacher told us" – he looks my way and nods his head to get my validation – "then why are the seats facing each other like it's a battle?"

Mr Bean's stuttering increased exponentially as he tried to answer. "Well…you see there is the ruling party…and they sit on one side…and the opposition…they sit on the other side…and they hold the government to account."

I explained to the children what 'hold to account' means. He thought that would suffice, but he didn't know how determined Malik was to get his point across.

"But our head teacher told us that it's the people that hold politicians to account by voting in a democratic election," he continued.

Mr Bean was not ready for that. "Yes of course you're right, but during their time in government they are held to account by the opposing party."

Then Malik persisted, "But how do they ever get anything done if they are constantly disagreeing? In school we have been learning about listening to understand rather than talking to be understood. It looks like they are not doing much understanding if they are constantly waiting to disagree with each other."

Mr Bean gave up. I think our time was over in the house and he needed to move us on. Malik could debate all day.

On our way out I told Mr Bean that we would finish here because we needed to have lunch and then catch the bus back to school. I think he was relieved that we left early. I thanked him and he congratulated me on their knowledge and insight into the process of democracy.

It was a lovely sunny day, so I took the children on a walk down Whitehall and then to Green Park where I bought them all hot chocolate after lunch. It cost me a fortune, but they were pleased with it. We fed some squirrels and ducks for a bit and then hopped on the tube. When we got back to school, the school secretary asked them what their favourite bit of the day was, and they all said in unison, "The 'posh' hot chocolate Mr P bought us in Green Park."

I laughed and said, "Yes it was lovely. It had marshmallows."

28 February

My indicative budget came through today from the local authority today and I almost had a heart attack. I have £50K less than last year. This is disastrous. School budgets are shrinking and not enough is being done to protect them because we are distracted with sorting out our national identity crisis. You tell me how I am supposed to keep all my staff, give them the pay rises, pay for increasing costs in services and goods and add more into the pension pot with £50K less?

Some schools have even started asking parents for contributions to keep afloat. Others are going down the road of redundancies and this will have an immediate impact on pupil outcomes. This is happening in the sixth richest country in the world!

My heart began to race when I thought about not being able to employ everyone next year. If worst comes to worst, we will have to stop employing two long-term agency teaching assistants. But they work with pupils with special needs and this means that our permanent staff will have to pick up their responsibilities. It's obvious how quickly it impacts on the children. Maybe all head teachers should get together and decide to run deficit budgets to force the government to do a U-turn and safeguard our funding. What are they going to do? They can't close all of us down. However, this form of revolutionary tactics requires a certain level of solidarity from the work force, and this has been beaten out of us.

3 March

Last night I started rereading Maya Angelou's book *I Know Why the Caged Bird Sings* and remembered something she said: "I've learned that people will forget what you said, people will forget what you did, but people will never forget how you made them feel." Before I heard this, I instinctively knew that this is what it means to be a teacher.

Do I always say the right things to children, parents, and staff? No.

Do I always do the right thing and are my actions always mindful of others? No.

Do I always make sure in the long journey we take together that I make every child feel valued, loved, and safe? I hope so – that has been my aim.

Suffice to say that being a head teacher is not easy. It's not easy having to define boundaries for people who have none in their lives. It's not easy to tell someone that their actions are hurting others, even when they can't see the hurt in themselves. It's not easy to tell someone that what they are doing is wrong or it's just not good enough yet. It's not easy to sit in a room with a teacher and her union representative and say that the teaching she is providing is inadequate and still need to look at her every day trying to struggle to achieve the impossible. It's not easy banning a parent from the school premises because they called one of your staff members a 'stupid bitch'. It's not easy having to respond to a complaint that is completely fabricated and give someone the forum to air their ridiculous claims.

We carry on regardless because we can see how we have made our children feel when they come back to show their appreciation. So, when I go home every night and feel wrecked and guilty for not having made the right decision, or said the right thing, I know that tomorrow I will have the opportunity to make up for it. If the scales of balance are tipped towards kindness and compassion, then we are forging healthy relationships that will make those we serve feel loved.

Today I made a point of going around in my learning walk to pick out those children that might not get some of our time. It's the quiet ones that just get on with things and don't demand so much attention. There are loads of those people in every society and every organisation. I picked them out and made them a big deal. I wanted to create a memory for them. It really makes my hair stand on end when I realise that this is what we do. We create memories that can last a lifetime. We are not always conscious of it and of course we can't be, but it's good food for the soul to go around spreading the love. I armed myself with special stickers and off I went.

6 March

Monday morning assembly is my moment to shine. In some schools, teachers ask to be excused to have a break or do marking during assemblies, but my teachers come for the entertainment factor. Today was no exception. I brought out one of my award-winning assemblies that I had in my repertoire.

This one was about Lent and Jesus's trials in the desert for forty days. I chose a pupil early in the morning to play the role of Jesus and told them what we would be doing. I played the devil and came to tempt Jesus to renounce God and follow him. I brought an arsenal of treats: ten massive Cadbury bars, loads of games, and wads of cash. Jesus must stand in silence and refuse to take any of it. One of these years I'm going to pick the wrong child to play Jesus and they'll just say sod this I'm taking the lot, but so far, they haven't.

I started my show and dimmed the lights and set the scene in the desert. Jesus stood in front, motionless and proud. I came out with a massive bag of goodies and began to tempt him. I love it when the children go crazy with all the things I take out of the bag. I started with the chocolate. Ten times he refused to take it, and the others were now delirious with anxiety that all this chocolate was going to go wasted. Then I took out some toys and electronic games and even an iPad I took down from the IT suite. He continued to refuse. The crowd were going wild. Then I reached into my pocket and took out a wad of ten-pound notes and started throwing them at him. I was even trying to put them into his hands and stick them in his shoes, but he resisted. I told him if he accepted, I would buy a computer for every child in the school. The screams were out of control and now the children were chanting, "Take it! Take it! Take it!" At this point I announced that unless he accepted my gifts, I would have no choice but to punish everyone. There would be no play time for a week. Carnage!

It was a resounding success. At the end I announced that since Jesus was so good at resisting the temptations, they would be rewarded with ten minutes of extra play time. They were jubilant. Everyone was rewarded but before I dismissed them one of the children asked me what I would be doing with the chocolates. I told him I would put them in the staff room for the teachers to eat. There was a big cheer from the teachers.

9 March

A little girl today gave me a poem she had written. I read it quickly in the playground and I thought it was lovely. I also immediately knew it wasn't hers. I didn't say anything to Samantha at this moment not wanting to embarrass her, but it bothered me all day. Later in the morning I asked her teacher what she thought of it and she told me that Samantha had been copying off the internet and presenting things as her own. We decided to speak to her together because she was one of our top writers and she didn't need to do this. She was also going off to secondary school next year and the consequences could be much worse if she continued plagiarising.

During lunchtime we found the opportunity to talk to Samantha on her own. I asked her about the poem and when she wrote it. She told me she wrote it last night. I asked her if she had any help or maybe was inspired by a poem she had read on the internet (this was her opportunity to come clean). She said it was all her own imagination. I felt bad doing this, but I persisted and asked her what a specific word she had used means. She didn't have a clue.

I didn't want this to drag on, so I told her not to worry and that we all make mistakes. I wanted her to understand that it was wrong to copy someone else's work and explained to her what copyright means. I encouraged her to write one of her own poems and told her that I think she could probably write a better one than the one she copied. I apologised to her if she felt bad and asked her if she was okay. Samantha agreed it was the wrong thing to do and we left it there. She was worried I would tell her mother, but I assured her that there was no need for that since she had learnt her lesson.

However, at the end of the day Samantha's mother came bursting into my office like a bull in a china shop accusing me of calling her daughter a thief. I was flabbergasted. I calmly asked her and Samantha to sit down. She said that Samantha was upset after school because her teacher and I accused her of copying a poem.

At this point the mother got very emotional and looked like she was about to cry.

"I watched her writing it last night, so how could she have copied it?" she said with her eyes welling up.

I was lost for words. "But Mrs X, Samantha admitted to us that she copied the poem. She doesn't even know what one of the words mean. I'm sorry that you are so upset over this. We didn't embarrass her or call her a thief, but we thought it was important for her to learn a lesson."

I thought this might help. Luckily for me, her teacher came for back up. I asked Samantha to tell her mother what she had told us earlier, but she denied everything. Thank God my instinct was to have her teacher with me, otherwise it would have been one of those 'your word against mine' scenarios. The mother was adamant and insisted that her daughter didn't copy the poem.

This was not going anywhere, and I didn't think the mum was listening because she genuinely believed her daughter wrote this and now Samantha was on a mission to get back at us for calling her out.

I wanted to put an end to this, so I said, "Okay, then let's put this down to a misunderstanding and leave it there."

Mum was livid. "No! You both (pointing directly at me and her teacher and raising her voice) need to apologise to her. If you don't apologise, I'm going to complain about you."

Well, this is one for the history books.

I chose the high road this time and just very robotically replied, "I'm so sorry you feel this way, however, neither me nor my teacher will be apologising. We were both in the room when Samantha admitted that she did not write that poem and we went out of our way to make sure that her feelings were not hurt. We did not call her a thief, nor did we want to punish her for doing something that's illegal. For whatever reason, she wants to deny it, and this is her right. My suggestion is that we leave it there and if you wish to put in a formal complaint then please go to our website where you will find our complaints procedure. However, I think causing all this trouble is unnecessary."

From all of this she only heard the word trouble and jumped up rather angrily and said, "Are you calling me a trouble-maker?"

I picked my jaw off the floor. *I was doing so well*, I thought.

I stood up and made my way to the door to signal that this meeting was over. She had all the relevant information to make a complaint, so now the ball was in her court.

After I debriefed the teacher, because I needed to make sure she was okay after the meeting, I went into the hall to join the extended school club for some distraction. I played some table tennis and was happily beaten by a ten-year-old. They are getting exceptionally good at playing this game. Then they all lined up to play me, but I needed to get back to my office and write down everything that happened in case Samantha's mother put in a complaint. Not only do I have to live through this theatre of the absurd, but I also have to waste my time writing about it.

15 March

"Beware the Ides of March!" I got a letter from Samantha's mother today, but it was only addressed to me. She told me that she didn't want to make me lose my job, so she decided as a good Christian to forgive us for our mistakes because this had caused her great psychological trauma and she had been crying every day since this happened.

I felt sad and horrified at the same time. There was something deeper there than the problem with the poem. I filed it away and decided to speak to her when she might have some more perspective on the matter. I was not qualified to sort this one out. I let the teacher know that the mother seems fragile, so keep an eye on the girl. She has been fine since the incident. She even came in with a poem she wrote herself and as predicted, it was even better than the one she copied.

I needed to teach year 6 this morning as we couldn't book a supply teacher and my deputy head was off because her daughter was ill, so she couldn't cover. They had sports coaches all afternoon, so I only needed to cover the morning. The year 6 teacher is so organised that I knew everything was planned to precision. I never needed to worry about her. We were doing science today and I decided to redeem myself form my disastrous science lessons of the past and prepare a 'hands on' experiment testing air resistance.

When I went to collect the class from the playground and told them I would be teaching them this morning I got cheers. That's always a good sign. If all else fails in life, I know I can still teach.

I told them we would be doing science all morning – designing and making parachutes to drop off the building into the playground. They seemed excited. I put them into teams and set them the challenge. First, we discussed what air resistance is and what materials would work better for the parachute and why. I asked them to make their predictions and write it all down so we can compare with the results.

By 11 a.m. we were ready to drop our parachutes and collect our results. We attached a little doll at the bottom of the chute. The teaching assistant went to the top floor with each group and threw over the parachutes. I was in the playground with the rest of the children and we timed how long each chute took to fall and observe how it fell. The children were taking notes.

Some parachutes fell slowly and others just crashed with a thud. We laughed when that happened and nobody felt disappointed. Overall, they mostly fell with some resistance and the lesson was learned. In class we went over the results and discussed how the parachutes could be improved and what material was best to use. It went well, and I told them that they could go out early for lunch. They cheered again.

Before they left, the teaching assistant interrupted me and said, "Excuse me Mr P, but maybe they should tidy up before they leave for lunch." I took one look at the room and couldn't believe I missed it. It was a mess. This is what happens when you stop teaching full time. You forget the sweat, blood, and tears it takes to make it look effortless. They tidied up quickly because they had the incentive of more play time and I sat there thinking how hard my teachers work every day.

17 March

Every morning a little boy from year 1 insists on coming in with his mum to give me and the school secretary a hug and wish us a good day.

Is there any better way to start your day than with a hug from an angel?

We are so lucky to work with children. Even when I come in sad or tired, they manage to lift my spirits. I know that whatever is bothering me will go away from the minute I step foot in my school. I think people who are clinically depressed should be prescribed time in a primary school as therapy. The children's needs are just more powerful than any drug you could take.

Today was unremarkable. I can't believe I had a quiet day. It makes me nervous that I'll pay for it tomorrow.

20 March

With so much competition between schools, we are forced into a preposterous situation of having to advertise to secure our numbers. I once paid £2,000 to advertise on the side of a local bus. I knew it was wrong, but I caved into the pressure of the governing body who wanted to increase our numbers. Recently I noticed one school advertising to recruit a PR person on a £30,000 a year salary. I wonder if the taxpayers are happy for £30,000 to go on advertising rather than their children's education.

I hate having to advertise the school in the local press, in cafes and flyers that we regularly distribute. I feel like a creepy estate agent having to show the school around to win over parents. This is unacceptable. I recently joined LinkedIn and although I understand the need to network and share ideas, I just feel it's all a bit of grandstanding. It's like Tinder for professionals: "I'll show you mine if you show me yours."

One head teacher recently gave a big shout out to his local newspaper for advertising the school. Why are we put in direct competition with each other? It's exhausting and diverting my attention and money away from children. Big schools have massive budgets and business managers to facilitate this, but in smaller schools it's all left to the head teacher. I once even went out on a Sunday morning in the local park, introduced myself to parents with toddlers and ed out flyers. Big Mistake! As a male they looked at me like I was grooming children. I vowed never again to fall into this stupid trap and just do well by the children we serve.

The other thing I hate with a passion (this is my soap box day) is when schools design schemes – most of which are cut and pasted from previous schemes – and then go out to sell them to other schools. So now we are not just trying to steal children from each other, but also make money off each other. Congratulations, we should be proud of ourselves.

22 March

I just got a call that one of our mums died yesterday. It is truly tragic. I knew it was coming as she'd been battling cancer for a while and had come to tell me about it. It's been a sad time. The child has already been living with her grandmother as the mum was admitted into a local hospice a few weeks ago. We have prepared ourselves with as much literature as we can get our hands on in dealing with childhood grief. I suspect it's the adults' grief that is more consuming now. Children have a resilient spirit. The educational psychologist suggested we just let the child guide us and she will show any signs of distress. However, the worry I have is what if she doesn't show any signs of distress? Do we speak to her about it, or do we just wait? What if she bottles it up inside and it comes out later in life? Will Grandma have the capacity to care for her during her own grief? Obviously, I can't answer these questions now and the psychologist is right, we will have to be patient and see how she reacts. My instinct was to try and protect her and it's hard when you realise you can't.

I called the grandmother to offer her my condolences and assure her that we are here for her and her granddaughter and will help in any way we can. She thanked me, but the words that came out of her mouth were lifeless. It was like the life had been sucked out of her. I don't think I have ever heard such sadness in another person's voice. May she rest in peace.

24 March

School council meeting today. My little spies gave me some useful information about what is happening at play times. It looks like the support staff are going back to their old ways. This consists of ignoring what is happening and huddling together for an extended chat in the playground. I have also noticed that a couple of them are using their mobile phones during work time. I knew this was happening because for the last three weeks I have had an exponential increase in children being sent to me during lunch time. It always starts when the weather gets warmer. In the winter they can't stand still for too long, so they walk around more to keep warm.

I know the drill by now. At lunch time I got my clip board and went out for my observations. It was more like a surveillance. I have three fixed points where I can observe everything and not be spotted. I feel like a secret agent. I do this a few times a year just to make sure I get a real picture of what is happening. Unfortunately, if they see you are coming, they scramble to do all the right things. Today was no exception and the scenes do not disappoint. There were three members of staff on duty and all three were huddled in a corner having a grand old time chatting away. I could see the children coming to them with problems and they very instantly sent them back. Today was particularly bad. They were ignoring some very outrageous behaviour and the children knew this because every time they did something naughty, they looked over to see if the adults were looking.

At some point a fight broke out between two boys in year 5. This had been brewing for a good five minutes, but no one noticed. It took everything for me not to go out there and give them all a piece of my mind. I had to hold back and watch all of this play out. They were sent to my office immediately; there wasn't even an attempt to sort it out and they all went back to their gossiping. I had instructed the school secretary to send any children straight back to the playground, so I waited for them to come back. When the boys came back, nobody even bothered to question them. They just went back to playing and Bob's your uncle. I continued observing until the bitter end of playtime.

My instinct was telling me to call them all into my office after school and give them a piece of my mind. I resisted this instinct because I was feeling angry and I didn't think it would come off well. I decided to meet with them all on Monday morning. This way I have enough time to consider my options. They have a difficult job to do, but there's no excuse for cutting so many corners. I was surprised they were still standing by the end of it. The biggest problem is that if a conflict at playtime isn't dealt with it just spills into the classroom and then the teachers are having to deal with it. For some children it can affect their whole day and they just don't learn. We need to get this back on track. Let's hope no one calls in sick on Monday.

27 March

I spent the whole weekend thinking about this meeting. C even caught me talking to myself at one point. I was going through my arguments and trying to anticipate what they might say because they are good at deflecting responsibility. But I had too many examples to share with them.

This morning I kicked off the meeting by telling them that I observed the lunchtime supervision on Friday and felt that what I saw was inadequate. I could see some faces go red immediately, though I wasn't sure if it was from embarrassment or anger. I continued to describe the things I had observed and read out my notes. I informed them this will feed into their annual performance management and as a group they need to make improvements immediately.

I invited them to discuss this and sure enough the first thing they did was to blame the teachers for not coming out on time to collect the children. This had nothing to do with their lack of vigilance for forty minutes. One even dared to say that there weren't enough of them out there to supervise.

My response was quick and held no punches, "I would agree if I had seen you all rushed off your feet not managing, but what I saw at some point was three of you huddled in a corner for forty minutes having a grand ol' time chatting away, while the children were left to their own devices. Actually, I think there are too many of you out there and will be considering redeploying some of you to work with the children inside."

This immediately squashed their argument and showed them that I meant business.

I continued, "As this is serious and any inadequate aspect of my school needs to be dealt with immediately, I have instructed the senior leaders to do a weekly random check and for the next four Mondays we will meet first thing in the morning to discuss any issues you might have and to review the progress."

I then proceeded to hand out an A4 observation sheet of what we expected to see in our observations. They have had all this before, but just like the children, they need reminding too. I spared them the humiliation of showing them the CCTV footage I had downloaded. I think the message was received. I know they will rise to the occasion and get back on track. I also take full responsibility for not spotting this earlier. It's interesting how people become complacent when they are not watched. I guess we all need a kick up the backside sometimes.

29 March

Today I had to pry two parents apart as they were literally playing tug of war with their child. What a great way to end the school day. I've had them feuding for months in my office and I have been playing mediator and marriage counsellor. I don't know all the details, but they have had some huge heartbreak and now they are taking it out on the children. I suspect this all started when the second child's paternity was contested by the father. I sometimes think head teachers should be given prescription pads along with their contracts.

The father only collects the oldest child that he believes is his own, but the communication is so fractious between them that they constantly argue whose turn it is. I've even put together a schedule for them in the past. On this occasion they both insisted it was their turn and by the time a member of staff came to get me they were each holding on to the child and pulling her like a rope. She was going back and forth between her mother and father and in between tugs they were hurling obscenities at each other. The child was crying hysterically asking them to stop.

I didn't even speak to them at this point. I just took the child's hands and they immediately let go and I took her to my office. My main concern was to make sure she was okay because she was crying, and it took some time to calm her down. Once calm, she explained that her parents were arguing over who was going to have her for the rest of the week. I asked her if she knew whose turn it was, but she didn't. She was adamant that she loves going with her dad and loves being with her mum too.

So here we have the reverse of what I usually encounter. Most single mothers are usually left on their own with little male support but here we have the exact opposite. However, they are so angry with each other that they are using the children as a ploy to hurt each other. I could hear them arguing outside my office. I excused myself from the child and went outside to give them a piece of my mind.

I was to the point: "I suggest you both stop talking to each other and maybe one of you should just go into the school office until I'm ready to speak to you. You've embarrassed your daughter enough today."

I waited until the mum went and sat with the school secretary and the father sat down outside my office. The child was clear, she wanted to go with her father and that was that. They have joint custody, and we have the paperwork in her file. On this occasion, she was in my care and it was my decision where she went. I quickly made a call to social services to talk it through and they confirmed this was okay.

Once she was calm, I let her go outside to play and asked the parents to come into my office. There was no more negotiating on my part. This had gone on far too long. I just let it rip. I don't remember exactly what I said, but I do remember at some point being so angry with them that I slammed my hand on the table. I think they were in shock, as they had come to expect a very accommodating and compassionate voice from me. Sometimes you need to give tough love. To their credit they sat there and took it like two overgrown school children.

I told them I called children's services, and this seemed to prick up their ears. I also told them that if they did anything like this again, then I would be making a referral and calling the police. I also suggested that when the father collects her, he needed to call the school in advance and he could come five minutes earlier to get her, so they could avoid each other. We would give the mum a courtesy call that he had collected her. They both agreed to this.

They are such nice people and I hated doing this. I have a lot of time for people who want to spend time with their children, but no patience when they hurt them in the process. What a day! I never knew I would have to play the role of King Solomon. I think at some point they were willing to rip her apart to win. 'I will destroy that which we both love so that you can't have it!'

Love is a curious monster.

3 April

At my approach to the school gates this morning, I got a strong smell of gas. Upon closer inspection I noticed that our copper gas pipes that run outside the kitchen wall had been ripped out. By the time we reported this to the gas board, we were worried about the children coming into school. We created a cordon at the top of the road and just kept the children away at a safe distance waiting for the gas board to arrive. At one point we saw one staff member coming down the road lighting a cigarette. The caretaker was motioning for her to stop, but she thought he was just waving to her, so she waved back.

"You better go and stop her before she blows us up," I said.

Thankfully, the gas people came immediately to sort it out.

Happy Monday. That was a close call. Within minutes word had spread and I had parents banging down the door demanding an explanation. There was nothing to explain. The gas leak was sorted, and it was beyond our control.

One of them asked, "What are your plans for preventing this from happening again?"

I wanted to say to her that I would become a caped crusader and go out on the weekends fighting crime, but I refrained from antagonising her and just said, "There's nothing I can do about random acts of vandalism, but I believe my staff and I responded in the best possible way to eliminate any risk to you and your children."

This seemed to satisfy her.

A few minutes later another parent came in late (in her pyjamas) and said, "Oi, the other parents are saying that there was a bomb in school."

I couldn't help myself, so I said, "Yes, but don't worry I diffused it before it blew up."

I could just see a confused look on her face.

I jumped in, "I'm sorry, I'm just joking, but I hope you realise that if there were a bomb in the school, we would not be standing here talking about it."

I told the school secretary that she could deal with the rest of the nonsense and I went out to buy some doughnuts to thank all the staff for acting so quickly. On my way to the bakery my phone rang. It was the chair of governors. Someone had called him to report their concern about the fire.

"What fire?" I said and started laughing.

I explained to him what had happened and apologised that he had been bothered for nothing. What on Earth is wrong with people sometimes? Are they just looking for a disaster story? I got back with the doughnuts and offered one to the secretary. It was quiet by now in the office, so we sat and chatted for ten minutes about how insane the start of the week had been.

"It can only get better," she said smiling. I know she didn't believe this, but I needed to believe it otherwise I would grow old before my time.

Before I left, she said to me, "You know, you probably could work for a bomb disposal unit. You have enough experience throwing yourself on them sometimes."

"Thanks," I said, "I'll put it on my CV."

6 April

It was our Easter service in the church today. It's always difficult to pitch it at the right tone. There is something naturally sombre about the crucifixion. Every year we sing a hymn called "Were you there when they crucified my Lord?" and the words always bring me a sense of horror at the sheer brutality of the act. I think I will change it next year, for something more uplifting.

The children performed an amazing play today based on the resurrection and they focused on the hope of the good news it heralded. The tone was right, and they were very respectful. I always get congratulated by members of the congregation on the children's exceptional behaviour in church. It makes me proud to think I have played a part in this transformation. Unfortunately, it wasn't always like this. Years ago, some of them would behave as if they were going to burst into flames when they entered the church.

The afternoon was a much brighter affair. We were having a whole afternoon dedicated to art activities. I walked around the school and saw some beautiful Easter eggs, chicks, and bunnies and even some Easter bonnets being made.

Last week we had some eggs in an incubator delivered and we had been expecting them to hatch. The most spectacular thing was that the eggs started hatching yesterday and the children had gone crazy for them. Last night I even went in after school and held one of the chicks for a few minutes. It was pure joy. The children in year 1 have been learning about life cycles in science and this has been a wonderful experience for them. They have drawn the chicks, written stories about them, made predictions and just have been inspired by the 'awe and wonder' as it is so often described in our circles.

Later in the staffroom we finished the term with some wine and snacks for the teachers. I always make sure I treat everyone at the end of every term. It's important for staff to feel valued and some wine and snacks go a long way.

24 April

My Easter holidays this year were like no other. I was struggling answering the question, "How was your break?" What should I tell them? It was like no other.

Upon my arrival at my parents' home in Greece, my mother announced to me that she and I were going to dig up my dead grandmother.

"Why?" I simply asked.

"Because she has come to my dreams every night for the past month asking me to free her from her prison. She was wearing black," she said.

"Okay," I said calmly, "but she's been dead for fifteen years, what do you expect to find?"

"It doesn't matter," she said, "as long as I know I have respected her wishes."

There was a logic to this process as in some urban areas like Athens the cemeteries are overcrowded, and people couldn't afford the high prices of graves. This was completely unnecessary in a village where there was plenty of space and the graves were bought for a pittance. However, in my village they tend to have this tradition as they believed a person's final resting place should be in a clean box with the bones wrapped up in a linen cloth. My parents moved back to the village they grew up in about twenty years ago. It was curious how two people who emigrated to America in abject poverty, managed to run a successful business and travelled all over the world could only feel most at home in the place they grew up.

My grandmother lived with us all my life. I don't think I had the best relationship with her because she was so much less funny and gregarious than my other grandmother. But she still managed to show her love to us in so many defining ways, like when she stayed with me overnight in hospital when I was ten years old because I was scared. She would treat us to McDonald's even though my father explicitly forbade us from eating there and it was our secret. She was a wise and strong woman for her generation, but that must have come at a cost to her softer side. She raised my father on her own when her husband died in the war and paid a high price for this solitude.

So here I am tasked with the macabre responsibility of overseeing her exhumation. My mother assures me that I won't have to do anything, and we will pay the undertaker to do it all. I reluctantly agreed. So off we went shopping for a metal box to put her remains in and a cloth to wrap up her bones. This was the most bizarre shopping trip I had ever been on!

After much debate on whether the cloth should be embroidered or plain and much deliberation on the quality of the metal tin, we purchased our items and headed back home. Early the next morning we set off for the cemetery just as the sun was peeking out over the cypress trees and flooded the graves with a brilliant light. We sat there in silence waiting for the undertaker. I was enjoying the stillness of the cemetery and it was a beautiful, crisp spring morning.

Out of the blue, my mum pointed to two graves in the distance and said, "Those are for me and your father. You won't have to worry about digging us up, because we will slide in the drawer," and she proceeded to lead me to the graves and showed them off like she was an estate agent. They were two massive above ground graves with an opening in the front for the coffins to just slide into the marble tomb. This was getting weirder and weirder, but I appreciated their foresight in wanting to make everything easier for me and my brother.

I asked her, "Which one do you want?"

Her reply was immediate. "I want the left one, because that's my side of the bed."

Fair enough, I thought.

A few moments later the young man arrived. He was very professional. He methodically took out his tools from the boot of his car and began his work in earnest. He explained everything he was going to do and talked us through the whole process. I asked him if he needed any help and, luckily, he said that the families should not get involved in any of the physical aspects. This was a relief because the last thing I wanted to do was help dig up my grandmother.

He lifted the marble top and placed it carefully on its side. Then the digging began in earnest. It took a good half hour before he reached what we could only describe as remnants of the wooden coffin. I tried to make small talk. But what do you ask a man who digs up dead bodies for a living?

I decided to ask the obvious: "What's the worst thing you've ever seen?"

He told me of the time the dead body had not completely de-composed, and the smell was so unbearable they were all spontane-ously vomiting, including the family. They quickly closed the grave and left it for a few more years.

By this point he had dug up quite a bit of the earth and he stopped and stretched his back.

"This is where I stop using the tools and just use my hands, so I don't damage what's left of the body," he explained.

He put on his gloves and went to work like an archaeologist carefully unearthing ancient treasure. At this point my mother re-alised that she couldn't take it anymore and ran away to the other side of the cemetery, leaving me on my own with the undertaker. Eventually he reached the cloth that she was covered in and care-fully lifted it out of the grave and placed it on the ground.

This is what is left of my grandmother, I thought.

I was not bothered at all by the scene. I had an amazing sense of calm and curiosity at the whole spectacle. When he unfolded the cloth, I was expecting to see a full skeleton looking back at me. The reality was much different. There was nothing recognisable. After fifteen years her bones were brittle and brown, much like the earth. All that remained almost intact was her hair attached to a piece of her skull.

As he was rummaging through the remains, I could hear my mother yelling instructions from beyond the graves. "Make sure you find her gold wedding ring. It's a keepsake and it brings luck from the afterlife."

"Don't worry," the young man said, "we'll find everything."

So then began the search for body parts and jewellery. He found her pacemaker, her porcelain hip replacement, a pair of glasses, and a comb.

"I can tell you like a doctor what operations they have had from what I find," he announced.

We still hadn't found the ring.

My mother kept on talking. "What can you see? I'm sorry I couldn't take it. Don't be mad at me for leaving you on your own," she said.

I think she had known this all along and that's why she had asked me to come with her. I told her what we found, and she wanted a detailed account on how everything looked. What shocked me most was that her polyester jacket and skirt looked brand new, like they had just come off the rack at Marks and Spencer. What a material. It would survive a nuclear catastrophe.

The young man managed to assemble a little pile of the bigger bones and put them carefully on the cloth we had laid in the box. He also found the ring and meticulously disinfected it and buffed it up before handing it to me.

Once all the remains were in the box, he said to me, "I will go and put my tools in the car. You take a few minutes, fold the cloth over and then close the box. We can put it in the grave when I get back."

When my mum saw him leaving, she yelled, "Are you finished?"

"No not yet," I yelled back (*this is turning out to be a comedy*). "I have to wrap her up."

"Make sure you tuck her in nicely, this is her final resting place," she announced.

Those words really hit me, 'Her final resting place'. The responsibility was huge, and I felt humbled that I would be the one looking after her for the last time. I looked at what was left and could smell the strong aroma of the wine that the young man used to wash her bones. There was nothing apart from the hair and the paraphernalia that accompanied her journey. I couldn't attend her funeral, so this was my last chance to say goodbye.

I tucked in the cloth and said to her, "Thank you for looking after me and always being so generous."

I held back the tears and closed the box. We placed her back in the grave and the young man filled it all in again and closed it up. I went and found my mother cleaning around her own grave and gave her the ring. She asked me what I saw, and I told her how little there was left.

She turned back to her own grave and said, "You won't have to do that with me because we won't be in the ground. I'm afraid of snakes, you know."

Now we had gone from the sublime to the ridiculous.

There was something strangely comforting in the whole experience. For the rest of the day, I felt lighter. I was happy to have said goodbye to a woman who had looked after me when I was a little boy, and even though she was hard and grumpy, she always spoiled us with presents and treats, and maybe too much love.

So here I was back in London on a Monday morning after an Easter break in Greece saying hello to my staff.

"How was your holiday?" they asked.

I smiled. "Very peaceful," I replied.

26 April

Nelson Mandela said, "Education is the most powerful weapon which you can use to change the world." I was always very driven to educate myself. I was a first-generation immigrant growing up in the USA in the 1970s. I witnessed first-hand what a lack of education meant: hard physical labour and a constant sense of feeling unsafe. Like most immigrants my parents were driven to own a business and following the normal clichés, my father eventually bought a restaurant. It didn't happen overnight, but within seven years of arriving to the country with no English or any formal education, he was running his own business. There was resentment from the indigenous white Americans, who now had to work for an immigrant, but this was a time of opportunity in the United States; an uneducated immigrant could take part in the American dream.

I was shown at an early age what it takes to make it in this world: hard work and relentless ambition to rise above poverty. I chose the route of education to my freedom and always believed that this was the way to achieve my own prosperity and fulfil my parents' dream for a better life. I was going to be living out their dreams; living a life of comfort and ease without having to toil endlessly to make a living. How wrong I was!

I now work as many hours as my parents did and possibly even more considering the head space my responsibilities occupy. I employ four times as many people and am responsible for the welfare and well-being of 250 families. All this for a fraction of what my parents made. Oh yes, I am living the dream.

But my understanding of education changed dramatically when my parents sent me to live with my other grandmother at the age of fifteen. This was not the one whose body we exhumed this Easter, but my funny, rebellious grandmother living in the 'motherland'. She was what I can only describe as the epitome of the Amazonian woman. Her poverty was beyond our comprehension. She was born at the turn of the twentieth century with no mother and a father who married three times after his wives kept dying on him. One of eleven children, she was never sent to school and forced at an early age to go out and work in the fields and tend to wild stock. This did not beat her spirit. She managed to raise four children on her own after the Germans burnt her house down and imprisoned her husband for being in the resistance. She was a true warrior, and I was inspired by her zest for life.

A few months after I moved in with her, it dawned on me that my grandmother was illiterate. I always knew it, but it hit me hard when I discovered her telephone book one evening whilst on the phone to my parents. I picked it up and was astonished at the system she had created to identify peoples' phone numbers. Next to each number she had a symbol or a picture to identify the person. For the priest of the village she had a cross, for the bakery a loaf of bread and for the bank there was a drawing of a coin. It was a magnificent combination of numbers and pictures, much like a personal hieroglyph.

That night I decided I was going to teach my grandmother how to read. She indulged me for a few weeks, and we spent every evening learning the alphabet and trying to sound out simple words. She was simply humouring me and wasn't about to learn anything I had to teach her.

One night while we repeated the same lesson for the tenth time, I said to her, "You know what, Grandma, the American Indians say that if you give a poor man a fish you have only fed him for a day, but if you teach him to fish you have fed him for life."

My grandmother stopped and looked at me with her infinite wisdom and replied, "In my village they say that a poor man knows when to bake his bread before he goes hungry."

That was the end of our lessons. I had nothing to teach this legend. She taught me that education is not what I think it is. She knew how to navigate through the hardships of life and treat every failure as another mountain to conquer. She managed to sleep in the fields and go for days without food and never lose her gratitude for the beauty of life. Every night before she went to bed, I heard her say her prayers to a God that she knew had kept her family alive. Seeing this made me believe that God was not somewhere else, above the clouds in some vast and beautiful universe called heaven. God was in this woman on Earth and in all that she embodied. When my efforts to teach my grandmother to read ended in vain, I learnt the biggest lesson of all: education is a personal journey and one you sometimes need to travel on your own.

28 April

David was in a foul mood today. He ran around the school for an hour while three of us followed him around to ensure he didn't leave the premises. Then at some random point when he wound himself up again, he took a cricket bat and threw it at his teaching assistant. It all started because he wrote the 'N' word in one of our reading books and wouldn't take responsibility for it. I tried to talk him down, but once he persuades himself that he is in the right there is no reasoning with him. That's why I let him cool down, but today he was on a mission to escalate his actions.

I'm happy to ignore children who are out of control, but where do his needs supersede the needs and safety of others? The balancing act is so fine when making the decision to exclude a pupil and I don't like doing it, but I need to draw the line when staff and children are put at risk. It doesn't solve anything for him, but I think about how others can react when I don't punish someone who has been violent. In the past I had a terrible experience with a staff member who took a complaint out on me because I hadn't excluded a child that had barged past her.

I understand that no employee should have to go to work and be physically assaulted, but those words 'physically assaulted' are not commensurate to an angry child that is out of control and barges past you. Some staff forget that they are children and don't have the same capacity of reasoning that adults do, but I sometimes find that the children let go of anger and hurt a lot quicker than some of the adults. This is where the relationships begin to break down.

On this occasion, however, I excluded David for two days. More than anything else it was to put on the brakes and regroup. I needed to make sure the staff were not disaffected. We didn't tell him until his mother came to pick him up and he just exploded. She couldn't control him either. My worry was that he would just spend two days at home doing nothing and come back even more wound up than he started. At least we had two days to plan for his return and try to win him back. Things were getting worse. Thankfully his 1:1 teaching assistant is a rare young man with endless amounts of patience and compassion. I put my faith in him.

3 May

David returned today. He was quiet and didn't make any eye contact at his 'return to school' meeting. I don't think these meetings are a good idea for him. All he wants to do is forget about it and get on with his day and here we are reminding him of his behaviour. Big mistake. I quickly wrapped it up and tried to show him some compassion. He loves table tennis, so I told him he could have some extra time in the afternoons if he had reasonably good mornings.

"What does reasonably look like?" he asked immediately.

I wasn't going to play his games today. "You tell me what you think it looks like."

"I don't know," he said shrugging his shoulders.

I stopped him before he could continue and said to him, "Before you remind me that I'm the head teacher and I should know…"

He smiled immediately at my pre-emptive strike and said, "How did you know I was going to say that?"

"I can read minds, David," I replied.

"You can't, because if you knew what I was thinking you would have excluded me for longer," he quickly retorted.

I was swiftly put back into my place. "You see, our conversation was reasonable. Try and keep it up."

He left looking brighter and I could see from my window that he was having a laugh with his teaching assistant, Frank. I crossed everything that he got through the day.

5 May

We had our school disco tonight and I am exhausted. My job every year is to stand at the school gates with a clipboard and check off the children one by one as they come in. It's a bit like being a bouncer at a club. I even wear a black suit and sunglasses and take that wide stance like my testicles are too big for my pants.

I sometimes play up to the role and say to them in a rather menacing voice, "You're not on my list, sorry you can't come in." I then just glare at them waiting for a response.

The more street-smart ones know it's an act and say, "Well you better check again." Some have even pulled down the clipboard from my hands to check for themselves. Never get in the way of a year 6 pupil and his disco experience.

Some of the more innocent ones look crestfallen. I don't keep it up for too long for them because it's heart-breaking.

The disco started at 5 p.m. and finished at 8 p.m. It was all the children could talk about for weeks. It was lovely seeing them in their finest. They really made the effort. It's also their first opportunity to socialise with all their peers in a more 'grown-up' way. Initially the boys and girls stayed away from each other. Sometimes they even stood on opposite sides of the hall like two camps of boxers ready for thirteen rounds. After a while, the boys ended up in the playground playing football and I took the ball away from them and told them to go inside and enjoy the disco.

The girls on the other hand were way more interested in dancing and gossiping about the boys. We only very occasionally get a boy and a girl dancing. They usually tend to stay in 'packs', a bit like adults do. We need to be extra vigilant with so many children on the premises. We only let them go to the toilets in lots of threes to ensure they are not being silly. It's usually the girls trying to drag the boys into the girls' toilets or the boys throwing water at the girls.

Once they had eaten and properly increased their sugar levels, we began a dance competition. This was the funniest bit of the night. For about fifteen minutes the teachers walked around looking at all of them busting their moves and judging the competition. It was hilarious; especially the ones that couldn't dance. There was nothing funnier than a child with no rhythm.

Tonight, I stopped the dance competition due to lewd dance routines. Whilst judging the competition I spotted two girls performing what I can only describe as an S&M routine. One of them was on all fours, while the other stood over her pretending to be whipping her bottom and pulling on her hair. Now this is something I can never unsee and it will be forever ingrained in my memory. I stopped the music and announced on the microphone that 'dirty dancing', is not allowed and I would disqualify anyone who did it. We promptly returned to the competition and things cleaned up. I also asked the DJ to ensure that the choice of songs was a bit more child friendly.

Later, one of the parent volunteers came to say that she disagreed with me and that the children were just expressing their cultural dance traditions.

"In what culture does a dominatrix whipping a submissive form part of a cultural dance identity?" I asked her.

She didn't answer me. It was ridiculous. I knew what she meant by 'cultural dance traditions' as some cultures' dance moves are more 'physically sensual', for want of a better phrase, than others, but what these children were emulating was nothing but the smut they had seen on music videos with young women being used as sexual playthings. I was having none of that 'cultural' expression nonsense today. It was wrong and no amount of spin was going to convince me otherwise.

After the dance I went back to my post at the gate to make sure each child was ticked off the list and sent home with an adult. By 8:30 we still had five children waiting to be picked up. This really spoiled things for me. We had such a lovely evening, and you couldn't help but feel unappreciated when a handful of parents failed to come on time to collect their children. Some didn't even apologise for their lateness. It was rude and it really wound me up. I tend to pick my battles carefully but tonight I wanted to make a point to one of them. She is a serial offender and always shows up late to collect her son. She never apologises and seems to have a 'bothered' look on her face as if we are inconveniencing her by asking her to collect her child on time.

When she rocked up forty minutes late and expected me to escort her son to the car, I waited for her to come out and collect him.

She was not happy. She slammed the car door as she came stomping down the path visibly angry at this inconvenience. When she reached the gate, she just motioned to the child to come with her and practically barked at him, "Quick, I'm going to get a parking fine." I didn't want to antagonise her further because the child was the one getting it, but I did manage to say in a very sickly sweet tone of voice, "You're welcome, have a lovely evening." She didn't respond and I was glad.

I got home at 9:30 ready for bed. I had been at school since 7 a.m. That's for all those out there who think that teachers rock up at 9 a.m. and leave at 3:30 p.m.

10 May

A few weeks ago, I was asked by the Department for Education to fill in a questionnaire about leadership and I decided to tackle it this morning. As I was filling it in, I was reminded of the head teacher's conference I attended recently with the theme of leadership.

This year we had someone from the corporate sector talking to us about how to 'grow our businesses' and motivate employees to produce more. This was particularly disturbing as we are now looking at teachers as employees on a production line and children as products we are churning out. The vernacular was changing. In the noughties they began talking about our children as stakeholders and in some instances, I even heard them referred to as clients. They are children not toys made in China.

However, as I was filling in this form, I couldn't help but think about what makes a good leader. It is said that bad leaders dictate, and good leaders motivate. I think the main problem with defining great leadership is that we are constantly trying to commodify something that is intangible. Are the best leaders the ones with the best results? This is what today's consumer society describes as great leadership. But it depends on what results you are looking at and how they are measured.

In my opinion, a school is successful if it is a happy and safe place to learn, where children and adults are supported to take risks and when they fail, they are supported to build themselves back up again. It's a place where success is measured by the quality of your personality and the journey you have been on and not solely the destination you have reached. Success should be measured in the quality of relationships and not solely on tests.

I've never asked my staff what kind of leader they think I am. But over the years they have volunteered their feedback to me, and I have been surprised by what I have heard. In my mind I am an authoritarian who values boundaries and discipline above all. I sometimes think I am a tyrant.

Recently one of my teachers said to me that I have a light touch as a head teacher, and everyone wants to do their best for me. What? Light touch! That made me worry that I'm a weak wet blanket and they just feel sorry for me. Though upon reflection I realised we were both right. There needs to be a balance. As a leader you must have the 'light touch' to know how to navigate between the authoritarian and the cheerleader. This cannot be taught. This is what we mean by emotional intelligence. So, until we stop focusing on building corporate CEOs to run schools like glass offices and instead invest in people's well-being, we will constantly be in search of great leaders.

12 May

At about 9:30 a very distraught parent came to my office to tell me that her daughter Sarah wouldn't come out of the car and could I help her. "Of course," I said and followed her out into the street. While we headed to the car, I asked the mother if something had happened and she said no. When we reached the car, I saw a very sulky looking Sarah who wouldn't make any eye contact with me. I tried talking to her, but she was very reluctant to negotiate with me. I sat in the empty car seat next to her and tried to gently cajole her into school.

"Did something happen with another child in your class?" I asked.

She folded her arms, turned away from me and just shook her head to indicate no.

"Did something happen with your teacher?" I continued.

Again, all I got was the head shake as she wrapped her arms more tightly across her chest.

I then tried to cajole her in, "If you come in with me, we can discuss this without your mum."

She continued her defiant stance and I detected a swift kick to the seat in front of her.

I persisted, "But you're going to miss out on the Flamenco dancing in assembly today and I know you were looking forward to seeing them."

Still nothing. Now she was even closing her eyes hoping I would disappear.

I stepped out of the car and mum had a desperate look on her face. This was something Sarah had copied from her older brother, who had done this a few years back. He has settled down now, but it looked like she was pushing the boundaries and copying his behaviour. Mum seemed to be at her wits' end because it had been a difficult time with her older son until we won him around.

"What if she does the same? I don't think I can cope with that all over again," she declared to me and I could sense by the way she was rubbing her hands on her face that she was about ready to cry.

"Well," I said to Mum, "there are two ways of dealing with this. We can let her have her way and you take her home, but I suspect she will continue this line of action tomorrow. The other option is to let me pick her up and take her into school. Obviously the second option is only with your permission."

She did not hesitate and immediately gave me the green light.

"Take her," she said emphatically.

"Okay," I continued. "You go into the car and start your engine and I will take her out. You must leave immediately, and I will call you once she's settled in."

It was like reconnaissance planning.

Mum jumped into the driver's seat and I could see Sarah was delighted because she thought she was getting her way. At this moment I opened the door, picked her up and took her through the gates. By the time she realised what had happened, the car was gone, and she was surprised to say the least.

"Come on," I said matter-of-factly, "you've wasted enough of your time and whatever work you missed you can do it in my office at play time."

She came with me without any objections. She looked defeated, but still wouldn't make any eye contact with me. I mainly wanted her to finish her work in my office so I could have a reasonable chat with her once she had got back to normal. I let her go into class and just announced to the teacher that she was running a bit late today. I watched her from the classroom door settle into her lesson and went to call her mum.

At lunchtime she came to me happily to finish off her work. She told me quite honestly that she was jealous that her brother got to stay at home when he was in year 2 and that's why she refused to come in today.

"Well, what do you think now?" I asked her.

She smiled broadly to show off her brand-new teeth and I could tell she was back to her affable, lovely self.

"It was a silly thing to do and I'm sorry," she said.

"No need to be sorry," I said. "We solved it. So, what did you learn today?"

"That you will pick us up and bring us into school if we refuse," she said laughing.

"Will I need to do that again?" I insisted.

"No!" she blurted out.

Revolution squashed and disaster averted. If only she knew that this was a one off and I didn't plan on repeating it.

15 May

It's SATs week. My deputy head teacher has been covering the year 6 class and it's been difficult without her day-to-day support on the management side. I have picked up so much more work over the last few months and I can't wait for these tests to finish. I've had to deal with most of the incidents in the school and that has really stretched me during the day. This pushes all the admin work to evenings and weekends and my work week has gone up to 60 hours. On most nights I wake up in a panic thinking I have forgotten something important and indeed this is how I feel on most days. My 'to-do' list is getting longer and longer and this feeling of constantly being 'incomplete' in some way is demoralising and draining me. Every time I think of something at night, I write it down on a post-it note and put it on the front door. I pick it up in the morning on my way to work and forget to even take it out of my pocket. I am looking at people blankly sometimes, just because my mind can't catch up with the conversation. I feel like I'm on a very tiny boat in a massive sea with holes popping up unexpectedly for me to plug.

But it's going to be an incredibly stressful week for the children and staff too. I never feel like our children are ready to cope with the onslaught of these stupid SATs tests. Once each test is finished, the deputy head and I complete an attendance register with the mark scripts. We must secure the tests in different coloured envelopes making sure nothing is missing, put them in another sack and label them for parcel force to collect. The whole process makes me feel like I'm securing the nuclear codes and one mistake could mean the annihilation of the human race.

We always tell teachers that assessment is about knowing what the children are good at and what they need to work on. If we already have this information, then the million-dollar question is, "What purpose do the SATs tests serve?". Especially when the secondary schools don't take a blind bit of notice of them and just retest them in September. Every year I feel like I am playing a very carefully choreographed routine to satisfy an agenda that is not adding any value to children's lives.

Again, my suggestion would be to divert this money (an estimated 50 million for SATs and 200 million for Ofsted) to school improvement. It is estimated that we could employ more than 5,000 teachers with this money. For the 32,000 schools in the UK this could mean an extra teacher in every school for 1 day per week. That's a huge resource for schools to use to release teachers to provide targeted support. I'm sure there are other areas in the civil service and policy making departments that could be streamlined to reinvest directly into the frontline services. We don't need more people talking about it, but more people doing the work.

19 May

The SATs tests are all done and dusted. The last parcel was collected this afternoon and now we wait until the beginning of July to discover our fate. We never really know where we will stand on the national stage because the raw scores are changed every year to accommodate how well or how bad all the schools have done. It's the blind leading the blind every year and schools are pitching it higher and higher in fear of being left behind. The national average rises exponentially, and the government proudly announces that they have improved standards. When it gets precariously close to 100%, they then dismantle the whole system in the name of offering more challenge and start from scratch to drop the national average to 50%. Then we have a new race to the top. Planning for this at the Department for Education must be a statistician's wet dream.

However, every year it feels like my job hangs in the balance with these results. If they fall significantly below the national average, then the local authority descends upon us like the dementors from *Harry Potter*. I have seen it happen so many times. Schools are put on a monitoring programme and head teachers are summoned in every few weeks to justify every second of what they are doing to make 'significant' improvements to next year's results.

So many people are broken at this stage and eventually leave the profession. Some I have seen spectacularly fall from grace where once they were the flavour of the month. This is when they send the 'henchmen' in to destroy reputations. It's all very brutal and Machiavellian. I have adopted what I call the 'Goldilocks' system; not too high, not too low, but just right. I keep myself and my school's profile just in the middle with only some flashes of success. I am affable to everyone that comes in and antagonise no one. I speak politely on the phone, wish people a good day and treat all admin staff (who wield more power than people think) with the utmost of respect for having to work with monsters.

I went to the pub tonight with some of my teachers to thank them for having worked so hard to get us through these tests. I was determined to buy all of them a drink. I don't know if it's my age or my lack of night life recently, but I was astonished as to how expensive the drinks were. They insisted we celebrate at a local cocktail lounge, the kind that have sprouted all over London. It was 6 p.m. and they didn't even have a happy hour. I went to the bar and bought the first round of cocktails for everyone and the millennial behind the bar announced that I owed £120.

"No," I said innocently, "there must have been some mistake. I only ordered eight drinks."

She replied, "Fifteen times eight is one twenty."

Wow. No wonder they couldn't afford to live in London. There was nothing wrong with my local pub where I could get my gin and tonic for £3 and at happy hour I could still get two for a fiver.

23 May

I arranged for some police officers to come in today and speak to the children about their jobs. It's good for them to see these professions as good role models, because unfortunately their experiences can be negative ones. A lot of my children have seen the police as the enemy. It's hard to shift their experiences when some have even seen family members arrested. This isn't the police's fault. After all they have a job to do and a difficult one at that. However, the discourse in the homes is that the police are corrupt and hated. We need to build some bridges.

The little ones were just fascinated with their uniforms and all the paraphernalia. They were good at showing off all their gadgets and letting some try the handcuffs, but their hands are so little they just slipped out.

With the older ones they spent a lot of time discussing the risks in our community and had a chat with the children about their fears and concerns. The older policeman was very funny, and you could tell he enjoyed coming into schools. He made the children laugh and had some hilarious stories to share.

But then the unexpected happened. During the Q&A one of the children asked him to share his most exciting moment as a police officer. He began by telling us that a couple of years ago he was on a team that were investigating a house in the local area where they suspected that they were growing marijuana. The minute he started telling the story I realised he was talking about a bust that had happened to one of my pupil's family, who happened to be in this class listening.

I tried desperately to signal for him to stop, but he was in full swing by this point and there was no stopping him. I knew from the police and social services at the time that the child was not aware this drug bust happened as he was staying with his grandmother, so he couldn't have identified with the story. But the police officer might unwittingly disclose information that could identify the pupil. So, I did the only thing that popped into my head: I went out into the corridor and pressed the fire alarm. That stopped everything and we even got a fire drill practise out of it; two birds, one stone.

On his way out I thanked him for his time and told him what had almost happened. I suggested he might have to stay away from sharing local stories in local schools in the future.

"You never know who's in the room," I told him.

He was shocked and said, "Thank God the fire alarm went off before I said anything that could identify him."

"You're welcome," I said, and he laughed.

26 May

It's the last day before our half-term break and I had an interesting letter from a parent today:

Dear Headteacher,

I am the mother of Star and I am writing to complane about the schools policy of giving certificats in assembly. My daughter only got 4 certificates this year and I think it is disgusting! She works hard and we put her awards up in her room and I can't belive your teachers are ignoring her. This makes her cry on Friday when she sees other children haven't worked as hard getting certificats for doing nothing. This is afecting her confidance and I am worried about her. I need you to solve this problem immediatly or I will complane to the council.

This parent doesn't even live with Star as she has been in and out of jail and is a drug addict. Star lives with her appointed guardian, her grandmother. I approached the grandmother after school to ask her what this is all about because I had never had any communication with the mother. She told me that she had recently been trying to cause trouble for all of them as she wanted to get custody, so she was making loads of allegations against them. I knew this was happening from social services, but I just wanted to get her views.

"Ignore her," she said. "She probably doesn't even remember sending it."

I asked her if Star was complaining about not being recognised for good work and she assured me that she was happy and content with the school.

I walked away feeling relieved that this was just the machinations of a drug-fuelled existence, but I also started feeling annoyed at the accusations. I decided to respond to her. It was more for my sense of justice than anything else. I knew it was unnecessary, but sometimes you just ride the wave of insanity.

Dear Ms Adams,

Thank you for your letter informing me of your dissatisfaction at our policy of awarding certificates in assembly. Our aim is to award everyone in the class an equal number of certificates. We do not all have the same abilities or talents, so these certificates are awarded for a variety of reasons. You state that Star has only received 4 this year. This is in line with our policy and she may even end up getting more than the average before the end of the year. Here is how it works:

We give 3 certificates a week in each class at our whole school celebration assembly. With 35 assemblies over the year that makes it 105 certificates we award. If we divide this by the 30 children in each class that gives us 3.5 certificates per child. Star has already received 4 and might even receive another before the end of the year. As you can see, she has received more than her fellow classmates. I have explained this to Star, and she seems happy that all the children are treated fairly and understands that we all have different abilities and talents to celebrate.

I hope this has cleared up any confusion about our policy and how it is implemented.

Sincerely yours,

Mr P

Head Teacher

As we have a week off for half-term, I decided to file it away and if I felt as strongly next week as I did, I will send it. I have loads of these letters that I have never sent. I always feel it's best to just get it out on paper and then sleep on it. It's the best way to avoid conflict when you really don't need it. It also means that I can have arguments ready if they do come back, so in a way it's my script for a second act.

5 June

My year 2 teacher informed me over the half-term that she broke her leg. This was a nightmare. I lost my year 6 teacher on maternity leave and now with the year 2 SATs tests coming up I would be missing my year 2 teacher. I sometimes feel cursed. It's so hard not to think that the universe has a vendetta out against me.

I went into school and prepared to start looking for a supply teacher to replace her for the long term. My heart sank at the thought of having to go through the pile of CVs and the endless interviews until I could find a halfway decent teacher to take the class. My deputy head is already teaching year 6, so I have no one to spare apart from myself. Maybe I should just go back into the classroom.

As I approached the building, to my surprise the front door was already open, and I knew it wasn't the caretaker having opened early. I see that it was my year 2 teacher in her classroom on crutches.

I opened the classroom door. "What are you doing here today?" I asked.

"Do you think that a broken leg will stop me from seeing them through their SATs?" she replied.

Most staff would have been off for at least six weeks. I was not expecting to see her until September. People never cease to amaze me. I knew she was loyal and hardworking, but her commitment impressed me beyond belief.

"You are amazing!" I declared and went and gave her a hug.

"Now what can we do to make things easier for you?" I asked.

"Nothing at all, just be prepared when you come in to observe that the children will have to come to me as I can't get around the classroom," she said.

"That's absolutely fine, but how are you travelling into school?" I asked.

She told me that she took a cab this morning and I offered to pay for her cabs. This was the least we could do for the loyalty she has shown us. This made her happy.

I went back to my office and breathed a sigh of relief that this extraordinary young woman was putting the children of this school first. I found myself quite tearful thinking about it. It was more the sense of relief, but also a sense of pride that this young teacher, who was one of my earliest recruits as a head, was proving to be an amazing human being. I was so proud of her.

7 June

This morning was bonkers. A mother came in and threatened our office manager. This had been brewing for quite some time as the mother thinks that the admin officer had reported her to social services. This mum was out of control. I had already sent her a letter of warning for her behaviour on the premises. She has called me a joker and told one of our teachers to fuck off. One day she even put her phone in my face and recorded me, while she was hurling abuse at me. She thought this was going to wind me up and I would retaliate, but all I did was just look straight at the camera, fix my hair, and ask her if I looked okay for filming. This was when she called me a joker. From what I know she has been banned from various public spaces in the borough.

Today her rage knew no bounds. She claimed that the admin officer was not letting her into the building and came in ready to pounce on her. I could hear the screaming from my office and went out to find her already behind the admin officer's desk getting precariously close to hitting her. We got her out and called the police. They told me to ban her from the premises, but I suspected that she would take no notice of this. All the police could do was come when they were called. We are just sitting targets sometimes.

Fearful that she would continue this behaviour after school I ensured I had two police liaison officers on site at the end of the day.

I stood with them, so I could point her out to them. I saw her at the end of the road approaching the gates and described her to them. At this point I left quickly and took refuge in one of the classrooms. I watched with trepidation to see how this was going to unfold.

As she reached the gate the police approached and she kept on walking completely blanking them. I could see they were trying to speak to her, but she just continued to head towards the classroom to pick up her son. I followed them at a safe distance because if she saw me, I knew she would lose it. For a split second I thought maybe that would be best, but I refrained from causing a scene. On her way out the police tried again, and she just barged past them. Apart from arresting her, there was nothing else they could do. I took my hat off to her. Now I must manage this insanity day in and day out.

For me this was a direct result of the austerity on the disadvantaged population, which in my experience I have seen divided into three groups. The first have taken themselves out of the welfare system through some means of employment, the second have just 'made do', and then there is a third that is just imploding. It is this third group where I see the children really suffering, and a change in people who are regularly smoking chemically laced 'skunk'. They are displaying the kind of rage I can only describe as psychotic. I have tried to be understanding and flexible, but over the last five years the parents I have had to ban for aggressive behaviour has risen dramatically.

One mother, probably the most vicious parent I have ever come across, told me to fuck off in my office in front of her child and other parents. When she couldn't slam my door shut because it was propped open by an automated stopper, she kept pulling and swearing until she ripped it out of the wall.

And why did she get so angry?

Did anyone threaten her or put her life at risk?

Were her children in danger of being hurt that she needed to protect them?

No. She thought it was okay to leave her son in school until 6 p.m. because that's when she had arranged a parent/teacher conference. He ended up with me in my office as no one could get her on the phone. When I told her that the school isn't just a drop off service and that this is not acceptable, she flew off the handle. Instead of apologising profusely and thanking me for not reporting her to social services, she thought it was okay to go on the offence and scream obscenities at me and rip my door off.

This is the kind of unpredictable behaviour that certainly urban schools are dealing with daily. From talking to colleagues in more rural areas over the years at conferences, I always get the sense that they don't experience this kind of immediate aggression. They get more micro-aggressions directed in e-mails at eleven at night that demand a response the next day. I don't think any of us are qualified to deal with such erratic behaviour. We've come to a point where we can't even speak our minds in fear of some unprecedented reprisal. Is it always down to poverty that creates these behaviours? That's the easy excuse. It does a disservice to poor, decent people who struggle daily to survive and don't behave in this appalling way. This behaviour is something beyond poverty and disadvantage. It is a cycle of behaviour that has gone unchecked and is not addressed.

I didn't ban her on this occasion as I am a firm believer in second chances, but I did send her a letter of warning. However, I banned her a couple of months later when she wrote a threatening letter to her son's teacher telling her to watch her back.

Who does that?

8 June

Just before the end of the day a social worker and two police officers arrived to inform me that they were investigating a family for abuse. An older sibling of one of my pupils had a deep cut on his cheek and his school informed the authorities. As we have the youngest in our school, they knew the mother would be here to pick him up, so they used us a base. I had no say in the matter and had to drop everything to accommodate. We had the meeting in my office so I could mediate if necessary because I had a good relationship with the mother. She already knew they were here, so she came into my office visibly angry.

They went through all the formalities and informed her that they were meeting with her because her son had signs of physical abuse. While they were going through all the protocols and sharing the information, I could see her getting angrier and angrier. I knew this was not going to go well.

It seemed like there was a heated altercation at home which resulted in the teenager being hurt from broken glass. The mother was having an argument with both her sons and in the heat of the moment a glass was smashed. She admitted to this and apologised for her anger. The sticking point was whether she intended to hurt him, or did he get caught in the crossfire. I knew that he had been permanently excluded from one school for bad behaviour and had only recently settled into another. I saw him sometimes when he came with his older brother to collect his little brother and we've always had reasonable chats.

The mother stayed silent all the way through the preamble. However, I knew this is the calm before the storm. She asked them if they were finished and then she suddenly just exploded into a hysterical rant.

"Take him from me!" she kept screaming over and over. "I can't stand him anymore, take him from me. I don't want him. Do you understand? I don't want him. Take him far away from me." She was jumping up and down by this point and beating her chest with her fist as if she were trying to exorcise some demon.

She was unstoppable.

I had never seen anything like this. My heart was racing, and I didn't really know how to help her. I got up to get some tissues to give her, even though she wasn't crying, but felt that I needed to physically signal something. She took a tissue and just held it in her hand while she was beating her chest and declaring that she wanted to be rid of her son. The social worker tried to calm her down, but this was only making her more upset. She pushed the social worker's hand away when she tried to console her, and she continued screaming and banging her fists on the table.

So, I gave it a go, hoping I could have better success. I put my hand on her shoulder and said, "We can see you're upset, but I have children and parents outside who can hear you, so please let's try and solve this together. I can't have you screaming in my office."

My tone was a mix of compassion but also a stern warning that she needed to stop.

She continued her rant, but at least she lowered her voice. All we could do now was wait until she ran out of steam.

This woman was clearly suffering something and adding fuel to the fire by trying to remind her of her conduct was not going to help. I kept on reminding myself that she wasn't angry with us. Too many people jump at the opportunity to shut down if someone is not communicating in a way they deem 'acceptable'. Obviously, what she was saying was horrendous, but it was coming from some desperate place and she needed our help. We needed to just let it play out right now and then build her back up again when she was ready to listen. We owed it to the children to think of them and put aside how we felt personally.

I moved my chair closer to her in the hope that my sign of compassion might make her feel more supported. I think she was surprised at the move and I could hear it in her voice, which was considerably less angry. Eventually she calmed down and at this point she really did cry. After interviewing her youngest son, the police were satisfied that the stories matched up and it was an accident. However, we were all concerned at the level of conflict that was occurring in the home and social services would probably be taking this to another level. It looked like the young lad's behaviour had really pushed the mother to her limits. At least they arranged for him to stay with his grandmother for the rest of week until they could put some support in place. We finished at 7 p.m. I don't even think I switched off my computer. I just grabbed my bag and went.

On my way home I couldn't help but think of how families can really fall apart in such spectacular ways. I tried to remind myself that it didn't matter which socio-economic strata you live in; difficult families exist in all forms. Sometimes teaching and learning can't even happen if we don't sort out these extreme problems at home. This is how difficult it is to get on with the day job sometimes. It has all become our responsibility and if I had the resources and skills, I would be happy to help, but most of the time it's like the blind leading the blind.

13 June

We had the school talent show tonight and it was the most well-attended event after the Christmas plays. Unfortunately, we are living in the cult of celebrity. Every year I make sure at least one child who performs with a musical instrument gets into the top three. It's important to recognise the hard work they've put in over the years to get to that point. Just learning a song for a few weeks is not equivalent to practising piano for seven years to get a grade one. Everyone thinks they will make it big with singing or dancing; it's okay to dream, but what if they don't? I don't ever want to squash a child's dream, but at the same time it would be irresponsible of me to pump them with fairy tales of unicorns and rainbows. I would like to show them that being a teacher or an architect or even a plumber is a dream. Talent is just 2% the other 98% is hard work with a sprinkle of serendipity. The only thing I can teach them is to work hard. The rest will be history.

Once the hall was clear and the stage was dismantled, we began the mammoth task of clearing up all the rubbish left behind. The scene was a bit like what you can imagine at the end of a film in the cinema. We armed ourselves with black bin bags and brooms and began the clear up. At this point a parent came in wanting to speak to me. I went out into the playground with him and he informed me that he got a parking ticket.

"I'm sorry to hear that but those bays are for residents only," I informed him.

His response floored me. "But I came to your school to see my daughter in the show. You need to call the police and explain that to them."

Are you kidding me? I thought.

"I'm sorry, but I don't think the traffic police care if you came to see your daughter or not. You are parked illegally and there's nothing I can do about that," I said as politely as I could muster.

At this point one would think that this would suffice.

He got angry and started swaying repeatedly back and forth as if he were in a ring waiting to start a boxing match. "You're the head teacher at this school and you're telling me that you can't help me to get this ticket cleared."

I felt as if I had just gone down some rabbit hole into a parallel universe. How on earth did I get here?

Believe it or not, I have a stock phrase for this kind of insanity too. "If you want to write a letter to the traffic police explaining the situation, then I am happy to confirm on that letter that you were here attending the talent show."

He was not expecting this, and it threw him off balance. That was my jab right in the kisser.

He was silent, so I took the opportunity to return from wonderland and said to him, "I look forward to your letter."

I walked away and thankfully he didn't follow me.

16 June

We have a pupil in year 2, Isaac, who is profoundly autistic and needs constant 1:1 supervision. His favourite pastime is to burst into my office at random moments during the day, run around my table a couple of times and then disappear. I always have my door open, so he has got used to coming in. Sometimes he stops and gives me a high 5 and I give him a sticker. It is our thing and I sometimes even look forward to it. He cheers me up with his laugh.

Today I had my door closed as I was having a meeting with some advisors, but it hadn't shut properly. While we were discussing some changes to the curriculum, Isaac burst in completely naked from the waist down and ran around the table a few times while we all looked on in stunned silence. His teaching assistant tried to catch him, but he was fast, so we just waited for him to run out of steam. After a few trips around the table, he shot out of the room screaming in delight. I could hear him laughing all the way down the corridor.

Do I even try to explain this to my guests? For a split second I thought it over and just said, "Apologies for the interruption, he usually keeps his pants on," and continued discussing the curriculum. All the people in the room had been educators at some point, so they knew what we were dealing with. It just felt like a bit of a farce to keep discussing how we were including complex needs pupils in the curriculum, when half the time we were running around the school trying to catch them.

By midday I had word that another application for extra funding for an autistic pupil was refused by the local authority. Now we would have to gather more evidence and spend more valuable time trying to appeal. It was clear we could not meet the child's needs without extra funding. He was working at a level which was three years behind his peers and had already been observed by the Educational Psychologist, who recommended extra support. The panel, however, wanted us to continue providing the support in school and collect even more evidence to prove it wasn't working. This mad no sense and was a monumental waste of everyone's time.

The reason so many of my applications for funding were refused was because we were going through a special needs funding crisis. The money was being cut and our staff were stretched to capacity. Beyond the lack of knowledge and training we also don't have the number of adults to cope with the rise of special needs. I worry that we cannot meet many of these needs and we all carry on without questioning if their placement in a mainstream school is appropriate.

Head teachers up and down the country scramble to make ends meet and ensure pupils are included. The biggest problem is finding the staff in the first place. Nobody realises that we can't just click our fingers and make specialist staff appear. Yet nobody wants to take responsibility or talk about it, because it would be taboo to say that some of our children with complex needs would be better off in special settings. We are doing them and their families a disservice by not offering them the appropriate skills to cope with life with relative independence. In the name of inclusion, we are excluding their basic needs.

19 June

I just got the call that we are having our Religious Education inspection next week. It's an important aspect of the school's community. We got outstanding last time and now we want to sustain it. Unlike Ofsted, you have a week to prepare for the inspection and this is a bit more human. It's a statutory requirement for all church schools and in many respects it's like a mini-Ofsted inspection. The inspector will only look at the teaching and learning of religious education, but they also evaluate the SMSC (spiritual, moral, social, and cultural) aspects of learning and the leadership and management of the school. So, again you are under the spotlight.

Let the games begin.

21 June

Today was one of the most difficult days I have ever had as a head teacher. David was out of control and it took five members of staff to ensure that he and the other children were safe. It all started at lunchtime during a table tennis match. He wasn't accepting his loss, so he smashed the bat on the table seriously injuring one of the children that was waiting behind him to play.

When he has done something wrong, he escalates his behaviour beyond any reasonable limit; it's almost like a distraction tactic to shock us into ignoring his initial mistake. I know he has no self-regulation, but I am responsible for the safety of the other children too. However, it doesn't stop there. In his attempt to get away from the adults he pushed over a year 2 girl in the hall and she cut her forehead on a bench. He then proceeded to kick over all the bins in the hall and threatened to kill himself again. It was very distressful for him and we were at our wits' end trying to calm him down. I really needed to put the brakes on this situation because it was getting too risky.

I called his mother and thankfully on this occasion she responded and came in immediately. I also called the local authority exclusions team to talk it through with them and one of the exclusions officers was willing to come and meet with us and the parent. I didn't want to permanently exclude him as he is in year 6 and there are only four weeks left in the school year. I desperately wanted to keep him in school, but he couldn't manage the whole day. Most of his problems happen in the afternoon and especially during the playtimes. I was stuck between a rock and a hard place and I hate feeling that any decision is going to have negative consequences. I had to make the one that had the least negative impact on everyone.

The only solution I could see was for him to be on half-days until the end of the term. He's usually okay in the mornings. We could provide work for him to do at home and his teaching assistant could even go and help him. This was the best I could offer at this stage and the local authority agreed that it was the most the school could do to ensure he would not end up in a pupil referral unit.

Unfortunately, his mother was unwilling to accept our offer and decided to take him out of school to teach him at home. This was the worst solution as I knew he would just be stuck at home with his mother, who wasn't coping very well. I couldn't believe she wasn't meeting us halfway. I asked her to reconsider so that he could finish the year with his classmates and enjoy all the celebrations, but she was adamant that this was not going to work for her, and she didn't want strangers in her home. I understood it would have been difficult, but there was nothing more the school could do.

It's emotionally draining when you tell a parent that it isn't working out. You end up feeling like a failure. But in this instance, I told myself that he only came to us this year having been to two other schools because of a breakdown in communication between school and parent. I knew she must blame us and that was the easy thing for her to do. I would probably do the same. However, on the positive side, we secured an Education Health and Care Plan for him, with additional funding that would continue until he's twenty-six. I know that under extreme circumstances we managed to keep him in school, and he completed his SATs and made good friendships.

She left with him and we didn't even say goodbye to him properly. I met with all the staff that were involved in today's incident to ensure they were okay and answered any questions they might have. I was worried about them too.

At about 5 p.m. I got a knock on my door and it was David's 1:1 teaching assistant, Frank. He came to give me his notes on the incident today. I could see he was upset, so I asked him to sit down. I knew that he was attached to David and saw him as a surrogate son. He told me that he felt like he failed him and then started to cry. I consoled him as best as I could and reminded him that David arrived with many complex needs and that in a short amount of time, we managed to get him a diagnosis and support that would follow him for a long time. We made sure, despite this setback, that he would now be on someone's radar throughout his teens and into adulthood.

I suggested to Frank that he got the children in his class to write him a card and we could send him some books to read and games to play. He seemed brighter by the time he left, and I hoped he would come back the next morning feeling better about himself. I also assured him that even though David would be home-schooled he could stay and work with other children in the school. The last thing he needed right now was to lose his job too. I will make magic happen and find the money to keep him on. These times are true tests of young people that work in schools. He's an intelligent young man and I know he will be able to make sense of this, but now it will just hurt.

I needed to lock up tonight, so I took the opportunity to just walk around the school and look at the children's books. It was nice to have the school to myself. The cleaners were the only ones left in the building and I could hear the hum of the hoovers busily working in the background. As I went into year 6, I picked up David's writing book. I made a mental note of reminding his teacher to send them home at the end of the term. As I flicked through his books, I could tell by the quality of his writing which days were good and which ones were bad. Today's entry was the worst. His handwriting was illegible, and he just ended up scribbling at the end. I ripped it out as I didn't want that to be the last memory of his work.

Even though it was dark by the time I left, I purposely walked through the park. It was a warm evening, and I didn't even need a jacket. The park is so well-lit nowadays that it's busy and full of people even in the evenings. I took the long route home to make sure I was tired enough to sleep.

However, I tossed and turned thinking of David and his family. By 4 a.m. I gave up on sleep and just went into the front room to watch some telly. At this point I remembered that I had the Religious Education inspection on Monday. Oh God help me.

26 June

The Religious Education Inspector came in for the day and we conquered. What a triumph! We managed to sustain our Outstanding. There was only one tricky moment at lunchtime when we were in the queue with the children. Inspectors always have this uncanny ability to find the children you do not want them to speak to. This was the case as he stood behind William waiting for his lunch. I tried to move him on to the other side, but he immediately struck up a conversation with William about the food.

All was going well until William turned to me and said, "Mr P, I went on a trip at the weekend to visit daddy and he told me to say hello to you." I taught his daddy years ago and this was not where I wanted the conversation to go.

The inspector asked, "Where did you visit your daddy?"

"In prison," William replied.

I could see the inspector quickly fumbling for the words to change the subject. He tried to distract William and asked, "What's your favourite subject?"

"Religious Education," William replied knowing he was the RE inspector and looking at me pleased he got that one out.

"Why?" continued the inspector.

"Because my teacher has taught me how to pray for Daddy in prison," William responded and gave me a nod as if he had fulfilled his side of the deal. I patted him on the back and moved up the queue.

29 June

This year's school councillors have been doing a sterling job. They regularly report to their classmates about what decisions we make at our meetings and how their suggestions are discussed. We also reported back to them at whole school assemblies and they took it in turns to show their electorate what changes they had made. They were particularly powerful when they lobbied for a new drinking fountain and I managed to get them a fancy one in the hall with cups and chilled water. That was a major coup d'état for them.

I took them to the local supermarket today to look at how products are packaged and how they could choose the healthiest options. It's been part of our work in promoting healthy eating at school. They have been selling fruit in the playground and encouraging children to make healthier choices. This was a direct result of a damning report from Public Health England where we were informed that we had higher levels of obesity from the local and national averages in our school. So now the governors want to see more work being done on trying to reduce these levels.

So here we were today at a leading supermarket chain and we tackled the fresh produce first. Our mission was to assemble a healthy packed lunch and present it at a whole school assembly. We were going to make a sandwich and then select some healthy accompaniments. We decided we were going to have cucumber, cheese, and lettuce in our sandwich, and I managed to entice some of them to try some baby spinach leaves.

Their knowledge of fruit was good, but they lacked any knowledge of vegetables beyond the basic salad stuff and some root vegetables. When I showed them courgettes, aubergines, and leeks they looked at me blankly. I know that a lot of these vegetables are an acquired taste, but it's only through constant tasting and experimenting that their taste buds develop. They were even surprised in the differences between some breads and we ended up with a nice brown loaf with thin slices.

By the end of our shopping trip, they got particularly good at looking at the nutritional information and I was glad to see they spotted the sugar levels in the flavoured water bottles and just chose plain water or milk for their drink. Our assembly at school was a complete success and they passed the message on to their peers that it's important to check before you buy. I know that we won't change all their habits, but if we can slowly begin to drip feed the message it might change some of their choices. That is the only success I expect.

3 July

I found some letters under my door this morning. I tell the children that if I'm not in my office they can slip any work under my door. I love it. It's a bit like Santa leaving me presents under the tree. They draw me pictures, write stories, copy, and paste copious amounts of information from the internet (note to self: I must do an assembly about plagiarism) and sometimes write me lovely letters declaring that I'm the best head teacher in the world. It does feel like being a rock star sometimes when I come into school. There's no other place like it. In the words of one ten-year-old:

Dear Mr P, I hope you have a lovely, magnificent, spectacular day. (These were the words on her spelling list last week…That's great.) You are the best head teacher in the universe!!!! You are kind and caring and always make us laugh when you read us stories. I remember in year 2 when you read us Dr. Seuss. I wanted to read it again and gain. You are the best!

Love,

Rachel

She ended her letter with a lovely portrait of me wearing a suit and tie, which I never wear. It's funny how children have these stereotypical images ingrained into them so early. Bless her. I will give her a thank you certificate in the good work assembly.

By 11 a.m. my day had gone well. (I'm in school at seven so a lot can happen in four hours.) I even had an hour to update the school self-evaluation document. No major disasters and most staff were in.

At 11:30 I made my way to my spot to have my lunch and half-way there I saw the school admin officer running after me.

This can't be good, was my first thought.

She got to me completely out of breath to announce that Ofsted were on the phone. They are coming tomorrow.

The rest of the day was a blur.

I ran back to the phone to answer all the trivial questions that the Ofsted admin officer asked. Her first question was how many children were on the school roll and I drew a complete blank. I couldn't believe the fear had made me forget how many pupils were in my school. I didn't even know what my name was by this point and think I had forgotten to breath. I could only describe the feeling by alluding once again to the descending dementors in *Harry Potter*. The closer they get to you, the more of your spirit they suck up. I could already feel vapours of happiness escape through every breath I used on this phone call.

Once we finished all the preliminaries and I remembered how many children were in my school, I was sent a username and a pass-word to connect to the 'PORTAL'. This is a bit like the matrix where you access documents and see messages from the inspectors. You are plugged into a world where only you and they exist.

I sat at my desk and noticed that my chest was rising and falling way too quickly for my liking. I now had two hours to wait for the lead inspector to call. I went outside for some fresh air and took in some deep breaths. How could this be healthy for anyone?

Only other head teachers could understand the sheer terror that these inspections cause. They make or break careers and offer little in terms of school improvement. Fear took over and all sense of perspective left me. I looked out at the children as they began to spill out into the playgrounds and felt an acute sense of purpose to do my best for them. I was their captain, and I would steer this ship through the storm tomorrow. Now I needed to break the news to the teachers.

4 July

So here we were. Ofsted inspection number six. The inspectors came in promptly at 8 a.m. and it felt like you were being investigated for a crime. I made the brave decision that I would challenge them to go for Outstanding. The inspector was new, so he was being observed by a senior inspector. Now I was in the matrix – an inspection within an inspection. One would be inspecting me and the other would be checking if he was coming to the right decisions. This was going to be tough. It was clear that he would have to cross his T's and dot his I's all the way through.

The meeting began in earnest with his lines of enquiry and the first thing he announced was that it would be difficult for a school such as ours where our results were only good to achieve outstanding overall.

That's when my tongue took on a life of its own and I said to him, "I challenge you to look at the evidence in all our books and see that our children make outstanding progress from very low starting points."

His response was immediate: "Okay, I will make that my fourth line of enquiry and we will look at the evidence together."

Success! Kerching! Kapow! Wham! Bam! Play it again Sam!

I was going to win this one because I knew that the progress in my children's books was undeniable. He spent the whole day observing lessons and talking to children. We looked at books together and I could tell by the way he responded to the children's progress that he saw my point about their rates of progress.

I kept pointing out where they were in September and where they were now, and I furiously flicked their books back and forth from the first page to the last. It was like I was possessed. I even heard him say, "I can see what you mean." I think he just wanted me to stop my manic fanning of the books. At the end of the day, he announced to my governors that I properly challenged him this morning, and we got what we wanted. Another two days of inspections.

"What?" I said out loud.

Yes, I heard right. He explained that he was not qualified to continue with the inspection to upgrade us, so a completely new team would have to come in for Thursday and Friday and start all over again. It just dawned on me that I would have to keep my staff going at this pace for another three days.

Bring it on! I am now Mohammed Alli; I move like a butterfly and sting like a bee.

5 July

I spent the whole day being a cheerleader for the staff. Everyone was happy we were being given a shot at getting Outstanding, but they were really annoyed they would go through it all over again for another two days. At lunch time a boy in year 4 had one of his explosive reactions to being out of a game and decided to smash the table tennis bat and stomped on all the balls so no one else could play. Let's hope he got his anger out in bucket loads today. I gave him some paper boxes to smash up later for recycling. Just to be on the safe side.

I was so worried about another team coming in to inspect us. The fear was palpable. You don't know what they might pick up on. Sometimes you feel that on any given day your school could range from Inadequate to Outstanding depending on the circumstances.

I quickly put those 'catastrophising' thoughts behind me and walked around the school to cheer everyone on and, especially, to keep reminding the children that we had two more days of inspection. I felt like I should have cheerleading pom poms. I had a permanent smile plastered on my face trying to show everyone that we would be fine. Before I left my office, I went through all the documentation that the inspectors requested to make sure there were no surprises. I learned my lesson the hard way in my first ever inspection as a head teacher. I usually doddle in meetings as it keeps me focused on what is being said. On one such occasion, I had doodled an image of someone hanging off a rope and wrote underneath 'My next Ofsted Inspector'. I only realised I had forgotten to throw it away when the inspector was giving me feedback and she placed the piece of paper deliberately in front of me to watch me squirm. I was in hell.

I got home early.

C looked at me quizzically and said, "Don't forget it's just a job. You are marvellous and I'm so proud of what you have achieved regardless of the judgement."

I got a peck on the cheek. I didn't feel marvellous, but I knew I was proud of what I had achieved. Too bad it always boils down to a couple of days of inspections and a set of SATs results for others to validate your achievements.

I wanted my children to say that they go to an Outstanding school, much like the three middle-class schools that surround me. I wanted them to be able to hold their heads up high with confidence that they were equal to those white middle-class children that have taken over their neighbourhoods. I wanted them to dream big and have expectations for their lives and go with confidence to achieve them. I wanted them to be happy.

"Are you talking to yourself again?" C said with a smile.

I was having this conversation out loud. "Yes, I'm rehearsing my acceptance speech."

"Good, then at least you're not practising the conciliatory nod of the loser."

6 July

I went in early. Incredibly early: 4 a.m., but I couldn't sleep, so I put myself out of my misery and went into school. I was wide awake at two but thought it would be ridiculous to go into school in the middle of the night. As if 4 a.m. isn't the middle of the night for most people.

I saw two massive foxes in front of the entrance and one on the roof. I jangled my keys and tried to make as much noise as possible to move them on. Nothing deterred them. They were getting cheekier and cheekier. I picked up a ball from the playground and threw it in their direction. This seemed to work, and I quickly unlocked the door and went inside. I checked to see if they had come back, but it seemed like they had moved on. I locked the door behind me just in case they have found a way of opening doors.

I checked the answering machine, but there were no messages. It was an unwritten law that you just don't call in sick during an Ofsted Inspection. It would amount to treason not to show up. I went to my office and made a strong cup of coffee.

I would really like a cigarette right now, I thought. *If I had a pack, I would have one right now.*

I distracted myself with my ritual of going around every class and sprinkling some holy water. I have a secret stash that the vicar blessed for me and I use it on such 'special' occasions. Anything to quell the anxiety of anticipation. It's this or the cigarette, so I chose the holy water.

The inspectors arrived promptly at 8:00 a.m. and met with all the staff. They seemed nice and told the staff that they understood that they had been undergoing an inspection for almost a week so they apologised again for the stress this might have caused, but reminded them that they just needed to do what they always do etc. It's a rehearsed speech, but necessary to put a face to a name. We went through the timetables and decided which lessons we would observe together.

This is the most gruelling part for any head teacher because you know they are also testing your own professional judgements. You don't want to get it wrong. You also know that they want your evaluation before they tell you what they think. Luckily, the lessons we observed were strong. I suggested we should see the children's books after the lesson to test the challenge of the work. He was most impressed I suggested this.

"Most head teachers don't actually want to continue once we have finished observing the lessons. This is refreshing," he said.

I could tell this tactic scored me some points. I was adamant that I wanted him to focus on the children's work because that is where we shine. It also gave me the opportunity to do my 'fanning' exercise again and reprise my role of the possessed head teacher. Pretty soon my head would be doing a 360-degree turn.

At lunchtime one of the inspectors asked to see a document I had never heard of.

I said, "Certainly, give me a few minutes to track it down."

You never say you don't have it. I ran to my office and called another head teacher and she e-mailed me hers immediately. This was solidarity in practise. We always looked out for each other. With all the best intentions in the world, there was always one document you had missed out. I cut and pasted our logo on it and gave it to him without delay. I dodged that bullet.

It all looked good by the end of the day and I joined them in their team meeting. This is the weirdest part of the process. For the sake of accountability, you are invited to observe them sharing information and reaching some preliminary judgements. As an inspector myself I know that this is bollocks. They have already discussed what they are going to say before you even enter the room. You are not allowed to contribute to this meeting, just in case it's contentious, but if it's straightforward then they are more relaxed. He recognised that I had been through a very gruelling week, so by the end of the meeting when it was just the two of us, he said that it was all positive and that the previous inspector made the right decision to test the school for an Outstanding status. My heart began to race and for the first time I believed that it might happen.

"I will finish early tomorrow as you have had practically a whole week of this," he said.

This was great for me. He asked for some evidence of the teacher's performance management for the following day and that was it. So far so good. Even the naughtiest children were on top form today. One of them even cracked a joke with one of the inspectors. Let's hope tomorrow he doesn't crack his head.

I went home with a spring in my step. I felt one step closer.

7 July

Last day. Almost there. Deep breaths. I went through my morning rituals (at a more decent hour today). I think I slept last night. However, anything could happen up to the point they leave the premises. It's a bit like in prison when you see them doing a lockdown. Although they don't frisk you, you do feel like you've just gone through a very intense interrogation. Hence more sprinkling of that secret stash of holy water.

Today's activities involved interviewing the governing body. Thankfully, I had an amazing group of governors coming in today. The inspectors observed a few more lessons and by midday they were finished. Now I had two hours to wait for the decision. Of course, they stayed on site until the end of the day when they deliver the 'verdict'. I just walked around the school ensuring all was running smoothly, trying to keep any disasters at bay, especially at lunch time when things could get rowdy. I intercepted a couple of balls that almost hit the inspector's window and carefully redirect a fight that was about to break out over a skipping rope right in front of their room.

By one thirty the children were all back in their classes safe and sound and I finally sat down to have some lunch. The lovely admin officer had made me a sandwich and gave it to me this morning saying, "I know you wouldn't think of this, so I made you a

346

sandwich at home." Bless her. I will always remember her kindness and support on that day. I sat in her office with her and ate it to show my appreciation but mostly because I wanted some company. I felt vulnerable today and didn't want to be alone. She gave me a hug and told me that I was a great head teacher and have built up an amazing school. I thanked her and I tried to believe it myself. Unfortunately, the imposter syndrome kicks in with a vengeance at times like these and I was still having my doubts.

At 2 p.m. the lead inspector came into my office and began his feedback. It was excruciating. He needed to go through each of the five sections they grade you on and tell you what category you 'best' fit into. If you get an Outstanding for Teaching and Learning, and Pupil Outcomes you are getting it overall. He started with Pupils' Personal Development, Behaviour and Welfare: 1 (Outstanding). I knew that would be the case. Now let's move on to the rest.

I just wanted to say to him, "Oh please let's stop this song and dance and just tell me what we got!"

I listened attentively and looked professional by taking notes that meant absolutely nothing to me at that point. All I was doing was scribbling nonsense. He moved on to Early Years' Provision: 1 (Outstanding), *Okay, I knew that one too*, I thought, *He's really going to string this out until the bitter end.*

I continued to write copious nonsensical notes. One of the big ones was next. Teaching and Learning: (Outstanding). YEEEEEEEEEEEEEEEEEEEEEEEEEEEEEEEEEEEEEEE EEEEEEEEEEEES!!!!!!!!! He sped up and quickly finished with Pupil Outcomes, and Leadership and Management: Both

347

Outstanding. He announced rather matter-of-factly, "So as you can see it is an overall judgement of Outstanding."

I took a deep breath to the pit of my stomach and let it out. At this point I realised that I was crying. It only dawned on me when the tears hit the ridiculous notes I was taking and stained them beyond recognition.

"I'm sorry," I said. Followed immediately by, "No I'm not sorry because this is how I feel."

He smiled and for the first time I noticed what a kind face he had. I think up until that point he hadn't even been a human being to me. He was the dementor. But now he was just another person and he really did look kind and compassionate.

He said, "Well done. I can see how much this school means to you and from what everyone has said, how much you mean to them. That was the unanimous sentiment."

I don't remember what else we talked about, but I think it was about how much I was going to enjoy the holidays without worrying about them coming in. He agreed. By this point I could hear everyone outside my office waiting to come in for the final feedback.

I don't remember much more of this moment apart from the smiles on people's faces as the judgements were announced. I thanked him and escorted him to the car park to make sure he was off the premises before I screamed in delight. My staff all deserved copious amounts of alcohol that evening. And to top it all off it was a Friday.

Once all the staff were informed (they tell you not to tell anyone as the judgement is confidential until it gets quality assured by

Ofsted and published online, but we can't keep it from the staff) and they headed off to the pub to celebrate, I texted C, "We did it! Outstanding in all areas." The reply was immediate. "Of course, you are! Now go out and celebrate."

The celebration was epic. Staff were jubilant and the alcohol was flowing freely. I received some lovely sentiments from staff who valued the guidance they had received from me all these years. I looked around the room at the smiles and joy and realised that this was my team – the dream team – and with all their minor foibles they had done an amazing job. I was the lucky one to have them working so hard, but it was joyous to know that they appreciated my support and leadership in this journey we embarked on so many years earlier.

I came home late expecting C to be sleeping. I was welcomed with a bottle of champagne, balloons, flowers, and a massive hug and kiss. Better than any Outstanding Ofsted could provide.

It was one of the proudest moments of my life made even more miraculous by the knowledge that it was achieved in a setting of the highest deprivation in the country. The distance I'd travelled at this school was monumental.

8 July

It's a curious Saturday morning. I think this is what Oscar winners might feel. Because getting outstanding in education these days is like winning an Oscar, especially with the challenges we face. I went for an early morning walk to get some coffee and muffins and as luck would have it, I bumped into another head teacher (of one of the middle-class schools). I was dying to tell her we had Ofsted this week and got outstanding, but I'm not allowed until the report is published.

As she continued rattling on about her upcoming trip to some exotic destination and all her amazing accomplishments, I looked at her for the first time for what she really was; an insecure individual who needs all this self-promotion to feel better about herself.

I let her rattle on for about fifteen minutes and decided I was going to rub it in her face. I didn't care what Ofsted said. I waited and I waited, and I waited some more, but she quickly flicked her hair and said, "I must be getting on with my shopping," and left without even asking me how I was. I laughed. This was her MO: get in, talk loads about yourself, don't engage with anyone else, and leave the other person feeling a little less important than you. I would like to think that somewhere in that routine she had some self-awareness, but possibly she was incapable of being vulnerable.

Not even this flippant woman could spoil my complete and utter sense of euphoria.

10 July

Today was the start of a new week and it felt wonderful. Now I think I can relax for a few years and enjoy a carefree time in my school without the worry of the dementors looming in the background. For the first time in years, I was excited to come into school today. It seemed like those Sunday evening blues were a thing of the past.

Pause for dramatic effect.

How foolish and naïve I was for thinking this! Within an hour of arriving at school I got a barrage of abuse from a very feisty mother who declared that her daughter Chanel is being 'bullied' and we were not doing anything about it. Back to business as usual.

She came in with re-enforcements in the form of a formidable sister who quickly imposed her authority by telling me she would stand there until I saw them, even without an appointment. She put both her hands on my door frame and blocked my exit daring me to say no. She looked like big foot.

I plastered a smile on my face, and said, "Of course I'll see you immediately – just let me rearrange a few things and I'll be right with you." I closed the door and kept smiling at her in case she got spooked and went for me.

I didn't have anything to rearrange, but she didn't need to know that. I stood against the door for five minutes taking in some deep breaths and preparing myself for the onslaught of complaints.

The euphoria had lasted for only a weekend. The heart and soul of the school continues beyond the accolades. The challenge is there no matter how many awards we win. Our job is to continue where we left off. There was no easing up as later that day I was reminded by one of the local authority consultants who said to me, "You got it. Congratulations. Now you have to keep it." I was quickly brought back down to Earth with a bump, realising the law of gravity: what goes up must inevitably come down.

Our SATs results will be published today and this might be the bump that sends me spiralling back down to Earth. I don't even know if we are above the national average as those sadists at the DFE won't publish the national average until later in the day. They leave thousands of head teachers in agony not knowing if they are going to have a horrible year spent justifying their results. I think we are just on the cusp. It could go either way. I checked the TES website for any information, but all I could see was an article about how head teachers were up last night waiting for the results to be published at midnight. For the love of God! Why would you do that to yourself? I only downloaded them at 7 a.m. when I came into school. I thought that was bad enough. This whole process is like an exercise in torture. I think they like to string it out to see which one of us will completely lose it. I crunched my own numbers for an hour and then shut everything down until I knew for certain what our future holds.

At about twelve thirty I received an e-mail from the local authority with the magic number. Alleluia! We were 2% above the national average and progress was average. That's good enough for me. The Goldilocks rule had prevailed. I sighed in relief that I wouldn't be one of those heads summoned into the local authority, shut into a room, and told that they will strip me of my dignity for the next twelve months. You know your days are numbered if you fall below what is called the floor target. That means you are below the national average for attainment and progress. That's like being told by the doctor that you have six months to live.

Last year I was in a head teacher's meeting the day after the results were published and one of the head teachers at the table looked like she had just seen a ghost. She informed me that she was just summoned into the local authority to have a meeting with the head honchos about her results. We both knew what was coming because we had seen it happen so many times to other colleagues over the years.

I just looked at her and said, "Don't worry, you will manage this and don't forget at the end of the day it's just a job. You need to have some perspective on this. Don't go in showing them any weakness. They will come down on you like a ton of bricks. Let me know if you need any help." Secretly however, I was thinking, *Dead man walking!*

I'm sorry to say I was so glad it wasn't me, but the fear I felt makes it deplorable that we put up with this crap. I have known this woman for fifteen years. She's a hardworking, decent person who cares so much for the children in her charge. She's been leading her school for many years with success and now this one set of results could define her career and her personal well-being. This is not helping anyone. But we are our own worst enemies for not blocking this insanity with industrial action. Our levels of dissent and constructive dialogue are non-existent.

I hope by writing this down and maybe someone reading it one day, it will be my form of dissent. I wish I had done more, but on most days, it was all about the children and keeping yourself above water. If nothing else, it's therapeutic to get it down on paper.

11 July

Today I began the mammoth task of analysing our data to identify our strengths and weaknesses (as if I don't know them already). One year's results mean absolutely nothing in the grand scheme of things. It's all about three-year trends now. If you notice a gap for more than two consecutive years, then you need to address it because you know that the local authority and Ofsted are watching you. It's a bit like the bespectacled eyes of T.J. Eckleburg in *The Great Gatsby*; the all-seeing, all-knowing eyes of authority lurking in the distance and waiting to pounce on you at your most vulnerable.

My analysis finished abruptly as one of our boys in reception class was out of control again. He had recently come to us from an abusive family and he was acting out. He was fine for the first couple of terms, but now he was displaying some extreme behaviour. I managed to get him into my office with the nursery nurse, but he was out of control. At one point he was lying under my table kicking it, while the assistant and I just held it down so it didn't flip over and hurt him.

When he couldn't flip the table over, he jumped on the chair next to me, spat in my face and said, "I'm gonna eat your fuckin' face!"

I was speechless. This four-year old had rendered me speechless. In all my years as an educator I had never seen behaviour as bizarre as this. The nursery nurse told him to apologise and he did. He screamed sorry in my face and then lunged at me trying to gauge my eyes out with his fingernails. I was powerless to assert any authority over this child who knew no boundaries. It was one of the scariest moments of my career. Luckily, the nursery nurse had a moment of pure genius and she began to sing to him, and this seemed to distract him. He eerily started to sing with her, and they went for a walk around the playground until he calmed down. It was like he had been hypnotised by the song and this was all very spooky. I think I could hear him singing in my head all day.

Once he returned to his classroom, I made all the necessary phone calls to report this. There was an open case with social services, and it looked like he might be taken into care. To be honest, I think it would be the best thing for him. The home environment was a mess, and the parents were not coping well and taking it out on him. He had seen his dad beat his mum up so many times he was numb to the sight of violence. He had been observed walking around the playground making slashing gestures with his hand and whispering, "Kill her, kill her." This was frightening.

I went back to resume my number crunching, but I couldn't concentrate. I was shaken up by the incident and as I sat back in my chair, I found myself crying uncontrollably. As I tried to make sense of my feelings, I realised that I wasn't crying because of what he did to me (although it was shocking to be spat at and told that someone was going to eat your fucking face) it is more about the realisation that this little boy has experienced more violence and aggression in his short life than I could ever comprehend. I felt powerless to help him as we couldn't reason with him. I decided to leave the number crunching and spend the rest of the day in the classrooms. I needed to feel useful again.

As I got home C asked me how my day had gone and as I relayed my experience with the little boy, I got this image of Hannibal Lecter in my head wearing that infamous mask and making that spine-chilling sound with his mouth. I started laughing uncontrollably.

C looked at me quizzically and said, "Why are you laughing? It sounds pretty horrendous."

I couldn't explain the insanity in my brain at that moment in time. It might have been my subconscious protecting me in some strange way by turning the experience into something else; something comical that I could process. I just hope I don't have a nightmare about it tonight.

12 July

In exactly two weeks I will be getting ready for the summer holidays. However, after living in the UK for over twenty-five years my bronzed complexion has turned into a 'whiter shade of pale'. I don't even look like I'm related to any of my family anymore. I usually spend the first few days in solitude at the beach trying desperately to get some colour, but while once I could adorn a decent tan, I now manage to muster a reddish shade of lobster. I think I just need to pretend I'm a British tourist and forget my Mediterranean roots.

I spent the day finishing off my annual appraisals with the support staff. It's so tricky to set targets for them and genuinely evaluate what they have achieved over the year. So much of what they do for children cannot be measured. It's about the care and love they provide to some of the most disadvantaged children of the country. Instead of focusing on that excellent care, we end up distracting each other with quantitative targets as if they are working in a factory.

I did find one of them tricky, though, because he doesn't take criticism very well and I needed to give him some home truths. I told him straight up that he had been rude to me when he didn't agree with my decisions and I had witnessed him rolling his eyes and sighing when he disagreed with me. I didn't have a problem with people having their opinions or even disagreeing with me. I welcome that. I hate this mean attitude when someone doesn't like a decision I have made because they fundamentally dislike the parent and don't agree with how I solved the problem. He failed to see the whole picture. I described his behaviours to him, but he couldn't recognise himself in the attitudes that I was describing.

At some point, when he was disagreeing with me, he even made the face and rolled his eyes whilst I was talking to him. I stopped immediately and pointed out what he had just done. He said he couldn't help externalising how he felt and that his family say the same thing.

"So, it is a problem that you recognise yet fail to do anything about?" I said to him.

I was quite frustrated by this point because his attitude was 'this is me so just deal with it'. If you are dealing with people daily, you need to constantly be aware of your responses. By the end of the meeting, I was not in the mood to negotiate or play coach with him. I decided to play the boss and just give him the target based on professional conduct and I made it specifically clear that this needed to be addressed. He left my office, and I could tell by his face that he was incredibly angry with me. By the end of the day my ears were burning. I knew he is slagging me off to the others. Oh well. You can't please them all.

14 July

The countdown has truly begun. It has been raining endlessly for the past few weeks. I can't wait until I get out of this miserable weather we have been having. I desperately need some vitamin D. This reminded me of an afternoon about twenty years ago when I was a classroom teacher and in the staffroom I said I couldn't wait to get out of this miserable weather and go away for the summer (just like the majority of the UK population who flood to the Mediterranean). One of the older brigade teaching assistants said to me, "This country has been good to you, so don't you dare criticise it." It was the same one who, twenty years later, put her hands up victoriously on Brexit day and declared her Independence for her and her nation as if she had just discovered it.

On this occasion, I didn't need to show any diplomacy and quickly whipped back at her in an extremely acerbic tone, "First of all Mrs Smith, I would like to know what you mean by this country has been good to me, because if you mean it has given me employment may I remind you that I am doing a job that neither you, your children nor your grandchildren are qualified to do. If you are offended at my exasperation with the English weather, then I'm sorry to inform you that it is the national pastime to complain about the weather, behind queuing."

She was so angry with me that she refused to come into my class-room for the rest of the term even though she was timetabled to be there.

Unfortunately, this xenophobic island mentality is what has divided us now and comments like "This country has been good to you" are quickly becoming violent attacks on hardworking people. I'm one of the lucky ones: male, middle-class, and educated, yet I sense the tide is turning. People are being xenophobic very openly now and racism is only thinly disguised at best.

As one parent said to me one day after the EU referendum, "Get your passport ready."

My response to him was, "Which one?" I'm sure it went completely over his head.

I couldn't handle being an immigrant for a fourth time; I don't want any more combinations. The only thought that gives me solace is that London is my home, and it is the most welcoming city in the world. I will just have to stay in my bubble.

18 July

Today we had the year 6 leavers' play. The children wrote their own play, and it was a triumph. At the end, I got up to do a little speech to thank them all for their hard work and commitment. I noticed some of the children were crying as they knew that these were the last few days that they would be together. Most of them had been together since they were three years old and their class was their second family; indeed, for some of them it was their only family and now they would have to leave it and go off to a big secondary school and start a new chapter in their young lives. I was also feeling a bit emotional as I had seen them grow up and some even called me daddy when they were younger.

Now I looked at them and thought they would be teenagers in a couple of years and the innocence in their beautiful faces would turn into something completely different. I was reminded of William Blake's words, "How can the bird that is born for joy, Sit in a cage and sing?"

While the parents were having their photos taken with the children one of the mothers asked to speak to me. I hadn't spoken to her since she called my deputy head a stupid bitch and I threatened to ban her from the premises.

I was nervous that she was going to have a go at me and spoil this wonderful occasion. I was wrong. She just gave me the warmest hug and said, "I know I haven't been the easiest of parents to deal with, but I know you had my son's back. Thank you."

It's in these surprisingly benevolent moments that we are made to feel like we have made a difference.

I hugged her back and said, "I appreciate this more than you know. Thank you."

We parted as friends and comrades on a common mission recognised by both. There's nothing more I could have asked for at this time of year. Thank you.

21 July

On my way to school this morning I caught myself humming "School's Out for Summer". It seems to pop into my head this time of year. It might be out for the children, but the school continues to hum away over the summer holidays. People don't understand that it's the time when most building work and refurbishments get done. If you don't have decent project managers to deal with it, you could be left spending your holiday worrying about the work and never truly unwind even though you might have gone away.

I try to get to that wonderful place where the only decisions I need to make in the day are whether I will go for a swim or have a coffee. It's a priceless feeling. I wish I could find a way to keep it going for longer during the year when times get tough. I guess it wouldn't be so special if it was the norm. So, the secret must be to see the special in the norm. I'm sure I've heard this one before, but it's nice to have your own light bulb moments.

The end of every school year is a good time to take stock in what has been achieved and how we feel about the work and the direction of education. The only problem is that I struggle to see the actual destination. This is what convinces me that the work we do is so often immeasurable and in constant flux. It's all about the journey. It's all about the relationships. It's all about the journey of relationships.

So, for the last day of term I focused on the most important measure of our success. The children. I joined them all day and witnessed their outpouring of unconditional love and this is where I caught a glimpse of our true sense of achievement. I often say to friends who ask me what it's like being a head teacher that, "It's like being a rock star." We are adored. But beyond that adoration lies a profound connection that cannot be measured in results or league tables.

It is this that makes the job of a teacher a noble one.

Epilogue – The Recipe of a Head Teacher

<u>Ingredients:</u>

Endless amounts of courage

Copious amounts of energy

Boundless humour

Oodles of empathy

High emotional intelligence

Oscar worthy acting skills

The patience of a saint

Sheer bloody mindedness

<u>Preparation</u>

Nobody can prepare you for what is about to happen to you; especially that useless qualification called the NPQH (National Professional Qualification of Headship). For a while it was mandatory to become a head teacher. I can categorically say that they could have taken that money and flushed it down the toilet. The fish would have benefitted more from the paper.

Don't go in like a bull in a china shop expecting people to follow you. You will eventually alienate everyone and have no one on your side; apart from scared 'yes' people. If that's what you want, then good luck.

Talk endlessly about your decisions with the ones you love. They know you best.

Your colleagues are not your friends. You cannot socialise with them without reservations. Go out with them, be generous and always buy the alcohol, but leave at a respectable hour when no one has said or done anything you or they will regret.

Never and I mean never give an inspector files that contain handwritten notes taken at a meeting with your senior leaders where you have doodled an image of someone hanging off a rope and written underneath "My next Ofsted Inspector!"

Always go out for a walk during the day for at least thirty minutes. You are entitled to a break. It is only a job after all.

Never compare yourself to other head teachers. We are all just feeling like imposters and some are exceptional imposters who make you feel inadequate when they talk about their achievements. Just keep your own goals in mind and stick to your journey. It is the only one you can be on.

Always forgive. There's nothing worse than holding on to ill feelings towards others. Forgiveness is liberating.

Never and I mean never blame the children for their mistakes. Blame the universe; it's bigger and stronger than they are.

Finally, you're a teacher after all. If you teach one thing then teach everyone to love one another. That's the biggest lesson of all.

There's no other job like the one of a head teacher. It fills me with pride to remember that I left some legacy in the lives of the children that I have looked after all these years. As I recount the qualities needed to be a head teacher, I always come back to one word more powerful than all the others: love.

I was recently coming home one evening and I bumped into an ex-pupil on the road. As she was approaching me, I was trying desperately to recall her name. I remembered her brother's name and even her surname, but her first name would not come to me. She looked at me, but quickly looked away. As we got closer, I knew that if I didn't remember her name, we would pass each other like strangers on the street. I knew she was waiting for me to remember her. As I looked at her face for the last time, her name flashed before my eyes and I called it out rather loudly. "Amaya!" I declared and put my arms in the air. She squealed with delight and told me that she wasn't sure if I had remembered her and was too shy to speak to me.

"How could I ever forget you," I said.

We talked for a while and she told me that she was a midwife and was coming back from a long shift at the hospital. She looked older than she was, but I think that must come with the territory of working shifts in a hospital. She had dark circles under her eyes, but they still maintained that girlish sparkle she had when she was a young girl. I was so proud of her. I asked after her brother and mother and she told me of their lives. She asked me if I still go to classes and read them the Judy Blume books about a boy called Fudge. I told her I certainly did. She laughed and asked me to do the voice for her. I indulged her and she squealed with delight like a little girl and clapped her hands like she was my audience of one. We were transported back in time and for a second she was the little girl sitting on the carpet laughing at my silly voices. She disclosed to me that this is the reason she reads novels. She said she tries to do the voices in her head, but they never sound as good as mine.

As we were saying goodbye, she gave me a big hug and said, "I love you, Mr P."

I wished her well and cried all the way home. Job done.

Postscript

David went off to Secondary School and didn't manage to have a great start. The school needed to put him on a part-time timetable to ensure that he could be safe. The same thing we suggested.

Ryan continues to terrorise his secondary school from what I hear, and I keep on receiving calls from social services.

Karen retired last year, and we had a massive celebration to mark her twenty-five years at the school.

Donna continues to bake marvellous cakes and inspires little toddlers to love school.

Frank left the school because his wife got pregnant and they moved out of London. He now runs a business with his father-in-law.

Michael was taller than me by the end of the year.

Malik secured a place in one of the most prestigious private schools in the country. His poor father had to remortgage the house, but Malik is now learning Mandarin.

Jacob's pre-frontal cortex has still not met his amygdala and I recently saw him shoplifting. I turned away and left the shop promptly.

Charlie is now working in IT and doesn't need the hubcap any-more.

Mary went to college and is now training to be a nurse. Maybe she will put her syringe experience to good use.

Beverly enrolled her little boy into our nursery recently.

Hannah got good grades on her GCSEs and went to university. I don't think she's studying horticulture.

Lucy and Evan are still friends even though he pulls her hair on occasion.

The little boy who wanted to 'eat my fuckin' face' was fostered and is hopefully out of danger.

Mrs Anthony and Mrs Brown never spoke again, but their children continue to be friends.

Ola and Maya learned to respect each other's authority and Maya eventually stopped her campaign to dethrone her. Let's just say they ruled in a coalition. I have not heard from them since they left.

Samuel's finger was fine, but now he is always too stoned to make any sense. I occasionally bump into him on the road. At least he puts the joint behind his back when he speaks to me.

Pat continues working at the school after more than thirty years and never loses her enthusiasm or efficiency.

Most of my dream team are still working in the school.

I am currently helping other schools improve (hopefully), and I have re-discovered my love of painting. I no longer look at my watch and wonder what is happening at school today, but my heart still soars when I hear my name in a crowded space and turn to see an ex-pupil all grown up. Those are the moments I truly treasure.

I was never able to ban glitter.

Acknowledgements

First of all, I would like to thank this book for keeping me busy for the first year I left headship. It gave my day structure and purpose and led me gently back into civilian life.

Like a child on its first day of school, I sent it off to some friends for their feedback. Thank you to all who showed it kindness and generosity and didn't send it back with a black eye. In particular to Eugenia Nterakopian and Dina Aktypi, who have known me the longest, and kept reminding me of the value of my experiences and giving me the confidence to carry on. To Rob Duggan and Alexandra Arlango, who gave their time to look at those first drafts and steered me away from my stream of consciousness (my own worst enemy). To Anastasia Valassopoulos, for all those mornings over Pilates and ranting and reminding me that it's okay to be vulnerable. To Pam Broadhurst for sending me my first review and filling me with hope. We lived those experiences together and your words of encouragement were the tonic I needed.

To Elizabeth Figueiredo, Jane Charman and Stephanie Edmonds, my dear Head Teacher friends, who told me that they saw the humour and the humanity in my writing. To Dee Whittaker for seeing the potential underneath my rough edges and teaching me the strength of silence. To Nelita Este-Wale for all the chats along the way. To all my colleagues whose love and hard work for the children in our charge made all the difference. To my family, who gave me the tools to be resilient and to never shy away from a challenge. To Nikki and Eva and all the staff at Clissold House café that I made my second home while writing this book.

To everyone at Vulpine Press who worked on this book and especially to Sarah Hembrow for seeing its value and giving it a chance. Thank you for picking it out of a very busy crowd and sending me hope.

Finally, to C for holding my hand when I needed it most.

About the author

All educators are storytellers. Tom finished a BA honours degree in Literature and Linguistics and went on to postgraduate studies at the University of Kent completing an MA in Modern Literature. Tom has been a teacher for almost thirty years teaching mainly in inner city schools. He considers his biggest achievement to have been the head teacher in one of the most disadvantaged areas in the UK and taking his school on a journey to outstanding status. He has also worked as a local authority education consultant and Ofsted inspector.

He currently uses his extensive leadership experience to support people in senior roles to develop their teams. His personal interests include oil painting, cooking (mainly Greek food) and still collecting stories that inspire others.

Printed in Great Britain
by Amazon

85778941R00222